# The Great Money-Grab:
## How the World's Wealthy are Winning in Real Estate

# Chad Anderson

New York Chicago San Francisco Lisbon London Madrid Mexico City Milan New Delhi San Juan Seoul Singapore Sydney Toronto

Published and distributed in the United States by: Plumb Publishing,

2825 Cottonwood Parkway #527, Salt Lake City, UT 84121

Chad Anderson's editor: Trisha Marshall

Cover Design: Joe Averett

This publication is designed to provide accurate and authoritative information in regard to the subject matter covered. It is sold with the understanding that neither the author nor the publisher is engaged in rendering legal, accounting, or other professional service. If legal advice or other expert assistance is required, the services of a competent professional person should be sought.

*-From a Declaration of Principles Jointly Adopted by a Committee of the American Bar Association and a Committee of Publishers and Associations*

This book is printed on acid-free paper

Library of Congress Cataloging-in-Publication Data is available.

ISBN 978-0-615-56566-8

Typography by Lisa Coldwell

1 3 5 7 9 10 8 6 4 2

# Contents

*"The most beautiful people we have known are those who have known defeat, known suffering, known struggle, known loss, and have found their way out of the depths. These persons have an appreciation, a sensitivity, and an understanding of life that fills them with compassion, gentleness, and a deep loving concern. Beautiful people do not just happen."*

*Elisabeth Kübler-Ross*

# *Forward*

I can't help wondering what my parents would be thinking right now. Born in the 1920s, my mother and father lived through many of the greatest upheavals of the twentieth century, from the Great Depression of the 1930s to the roaring recovery of the decades that followed the Second World War. Both grew up in homes where they had to share houses with other families, absent of indoor plumbing and refrigerators. They recounted stories of the bread lines and tent cities and government-issued clothing that marked the urban misery of the Depression years. My father remembers the embarrassment of wearing the government clothes to school and having other kids make fun of him. In 1941, my dad left home at age 15, lied about his age, and joined the U.S. Navy just to have regular meals and a real uniform. He had never seen the ocean before and was sent by aircraft carrier to Japan where he fought in Okinawa and Saipan. He loved the U.S. and the life we have. My mother tells stories of saving wrapping paper as a child after living through the Great Depression. But thirty years later, they were able to follow countless contemporaries to the greener pastures of the suburbs, buying their first house on their own, then a shiny new Chevrolet, a washing machine, and a television, and raising their children in relative security. My father saw his low-wage job turn into a sales manager job, which was high paying work that could support our entire family.

Every society experiences ups and downs in their economy, just like my parents did. When the economy gets tough it can be difficult, sometimes horribly painful, but just like our bodies are always replenishing our cells and making room for new growth, economies restart themselves. The cycles of economies educate us on what is not working and we learn to improve our skills and perfect the power behind the economy which is its people. During the 1870s and 1880s, we saw the rise of mass public education, which provided an immigrant workforce with basic reading and math skills necessary to allow factories to grow and prosper. The Great Depression created the groundwork to necessitate the opportunity for the G.I. Bill and made higher education possible for the masses after World War II, economically uplifting a whole generation. As a society, we've learned that crises forces us all use our human talent better and improve our economics in the process.

One thing I've learned writing this book is how people changing the way they live, can change economic cycles and it's not always about government policies and programs that cause economic cycles. The economic crisis we are currently experiencing is showing us how to achieve a more meaningful and sustainable way of life through our beliefs and habits; it's made us value the idea that we don't need to define ourselves in terms of our "stuff". We've learned that we need to live within our means and to stay out of debt.

In my conversations, I've heard from people who are in the process of resetting their lives. Young people just out of college tell me that they don't want their parents' suburban lifestyle; they'd prefer to find an affordable rental or townhome in a city they love, where economic opportunities are better. They don't want to go into hock buying a big house and a big car just so they can endure a long commute. Young parents say they've had to defer their dream of buying a bigger house with a backyard, either because they can't afford it or because they don't qualify for a mortgage. Empty nesters tell me they've decided to sell the big house, sometimes for a lot less than they could have gotten a few years ago, and buy a smaller condo or house closer to their kids. This subtle shift, brought on by economic circumstances, is bringing about a gradual but enduring change in the way we live – one that will prove every bit as consequential as the move toward suburban living in the 1950s and 1960s.

However, our politicians and CEOs are behind the times. The average American has already slowed spending and has been forced to face the economic music, while our leaders are still refusing to engage in the economic transformation. Our leaders are living in the past, believing that things will come back as they once were and we see it in their efforts to revive the broken banking systems, land sprawl, and the inefficient and energy wasting way of life that was the underlying cause of the crisis.

The U.S. job machine has not only sputtered, it has nearly died. According to Bureau of Labor Statistics projections, the U.S. economy remains on track to generate 15 million new jobs over the next decade. Roughly half of those new jobs – 6.8 million of them – will be high-skill, high–wage work in the knowledge, professional, and technical sectors of the economy. The other half will be much lower-paying, low-skill work in the routine service sector of the economy. More than 45 percent of the U.S. workforce – sixty million workers – already do this kind of work. These service workers, who prepare our food, take care of our homes earn only a third of what professional, technical, and knowledge workers are paid.

It is as though we have had a broken leg and the doctor put a band-aid on our leg. We now have a choice to walk around with an inefficient limb, or break the leg again and start over with the hopes of having a great leg in the future. The band-aid has been three years of easy banking credit, targeted stimulus, and government playing innovator.

The past worked for us economically for a long time, but the world has different needs now and the opportunities are endless, especially in providing housing for the extra 100 million people joining the U.S. population both from birth and immigration. This much demand will be the greatest opportunity to gain wealth back that was lost over the past 10 years. There is no stopping the reset. My hope is that this book will help you move more quickly to the opportunities you feel comfortable with and usher in a new era of shared and sustainable prosperity.

Chad Anderson

# THE PAST

# Chapter 1: The Result of Government Spending

What we are learning is that financially things are worse than we thought and we're headed down from here.

But, instinctively we knew that, because in our own homes, we know you can't keep going deeper in debt forever. But in this economic downturn, we have two things that are different. First, these arguments are being played out in the media followed up with a lot of research by Americans on the Internet. Second, there is a feeling that there is no way out of the current situation.

It's easy to get confused about what has been going on in the economy. Currently, the stock market is all over the board, up one day and down the next. Just when it seems as though the economy is improving, news comes out to show that we are headed into another recession. And while all this is going on, many people are just living their lives like nothing has happened.

Keep this statistic in mind as you compare the current situation in the United States to what has turned to chaos in Greece: If you add municipal debt to the official national debt of the U.S., the total is already at Greek levels of about 120% of GDP.

The Republican Party used to be what we refer to as fiscally conservative. However, they broke from that when they started following Keynesianism policies, in which deficits don't matter because the economy will expand and that will naturally make the deficit small as a percentage of GDP. The policies include cutting taxes to boost GDP and thereby increasing tax receipts.

The Reagan-era cuts seemed to pay off. The economy boomed. Republicans believed they had the winning formula: promise voters the moon and count on supply-side growth to pay for it. But the boom of the '80s and '90s was really Paul Volcker's victory…not a victory for Republican fiscal management. After Volcker got control of inflation, the economy was able to grow and prosper for the next 20 years as interest rates fell and stocks rose.

The "deficits don't matter" creed backfired under the administration of George W Bush. Spending programs – projected into the future – created huge structural deficit gaps that cannot now be closed by any reasonable economic growth assumptions.

But that's not all. The government deficit is only part of the problem as there is now a trade deficit of $8 trillion – money spent by the public on goods and services purchased oversees and not offset by investment back into the US by means of higher exports.

Official federal debt and the accumulated trade shortfalls adds up to $26 trillion – not quite 200% of GDP, but getting there.

Our discipline has gone out the window and now all we have is global monetary chaos as foreign central banks run their own printing presses at even faster speeds to keep up with the tidal wave of dollars coming from the Federal Reserve.

The combined assets of conventional banks and the so-called shadow banking system (including investment banks and finance companies) grew from a mere $500 billion in 1970 to $30 trillion by September 2008.

But the trillion-dollar conglomerates that inhabit this new financial world are not free enterprises. They are rather wards of the state, extracting billions from the economy with a lot of pointless speculation in stocks, bonds, commodities and derivatives. They could never have survived, much less thrived, if their deposits had not been government-guaranteed and if they hadn't been able to obtain virtually free money from the Fed's discount window to cover their bad bets.

The United States has been headed in this direction for a long time, but it's time to face the music – we're broke. Spending more or taxing less won't get us out of this mess and allow us to pay our bills.

## Lessons from the Depression

Going back to the Great Depression of the 1930s, history reminds us there was a real estate bubble, also fueled by loose lending standards and small down payments required by lenders. The real estate problems back then are the same ones we are facing today.

In the mid 1920s, Florida real estate was the spot for speculation. Developers figured out they could charge more for homes by decreasing the amount buyers had to put down on a home. At the time, normal down payments were 50% of the loan and the term was five years, but by decreasing that to a shocking 10% down was very enticing to potential buyers.

The risky loans went bad first, but it was the spread of credit problems to the supposedly safe loans — five years and 50% down — that caused the housing market to collapse.

One of the interesting things about the five year loans, is that no payments were required (similar to interest only loans of today) to reduce principle. However, the buyer had to refinance at the end of the five years. However, the stock market crash made it impossible for people to borrow and nobody could refinance – just like the liquidity crisis of today.

Millions of homes were foreclosed on. Falling prices on everything from homes to farm crops to wages, made consumers hesitant to buy anything and even if they wanted to banks were afraid to lend money on assets that were going down in value.

As part of the New Deal, the government took control of millions of loans and restructured them into something new: the modern mortgage, with 20% down and principal that is repaid over the life of the loan. The government extended the mortgages to 15 years, then 25 and finally 30.

When World War II ended in 1945 and the Baby Boom began the following year, the 30-year, fixed-rate mortgage became a cornerstone of society and led to unprecedented levels of homeownership.

## *Key Points from this Chapter*

- When World War II ended in 1945 and the Baby Boom began the following year, the 30-year, fixed-rate mortgage became a cornerstone of society and led to unprecedented levels of homeownership.
- The Great Depression of the 1930s was preceded by a real estate bubble, also fueled by loose lending standards and shrinking down payment requirements. Those real estate problems — and solutions — echo today's.
- Millions of families lost their homes to foreclosure. Falling prices on nearly everything — homes, farm crops, wages — made consumers reluctant to buy and banks afraid to lend.
- As part of the New Deal, the government took control of millions of loans and restructured them into something new: the modern mortgage, with 20% down and principal that is repaid over the life of the loan. The government extended the mortgages to 15 years, then 25 and finally 30.

# Chapter 2:  A 50 Year History of Stable Prices

Until recently, homes were stable, unspectacular investments, not get-rich-quick schemes.

**Home prices as a mulitple of income**

— Media ratio of home price to income
— Average ratio of home price to income

Source: Census Bureau, S&P/Case-Shiller Home Price Indices

**The history of housing as an investment**

Home prices (in thousands of dollars)

Source: Economist Robert Shiller, Yale University

Nationally, the typical existing home was worth roughly the same in 2000 as it was in 1950, after adjusting for inflation.

The new homes being built were larger and more expensive than the existing, older homes of the time. As time passed, that translated to Americans living in larger, more valuable homes overall. But homes grew slowly in value, with the exceptions being California and Texas in the 70s and 80s and Florida at certain times over a century period.

Even though home values only increased modestly, homes were still considered smart investments. Owners lived in a house, and then owned it at the end of the mortgage period as compared to renting where they had no equity. Borrowers got tax breaks as well and built equity that could be leveraged into bigger houses as their incomes grew.

The boom lasted from 2002 to 2006, when houses went from being a slow investment to an incredible investment. Home sale profits and relaxed lending standards such as lower down payment requirements and adjustable-rate mortgages (ARMs) made it possible for buyers of all income levels to pay more for houses.

But when the housing bubble began to end in 2006, we learned a lesson. Home values had closely tracked three common-sense measures for many years:

- **Income** —Home values floated at about three times average household income from 1950 to 2000. In 2006, the average household income was $66,500. Under the traditional model, home prices should have been about $200,000. Instead, the typical home sold for $301,000.

- **Rent** —Homes traditionally have sold for about 20 times what it would cost to rent them for a year. In 2006, houses were selling for 32 times annual rent.

- **Appreciation** —Existing homes grew in value by less than 0.5% per year, after adjusting for inflation, from 1950 to 2000. From 2000 to 2006, home prices rose at an average annualized rate of 8.2% above inflation and peaked with a 12.3% jump in 2005. Housing prices began to fall in the second quarter of 2006.

Inflation could help homes recapture their old prices, if not their value. But when inflation is factored in, home prices might not return to their 2006 peak for many years. Housing prices are meaningless if you don't adjust for inflation.

Gold peaked in 1980 at $850 an ounce in response to inflation and the Iranian hostage crisis. It never recovered. Today, it sells for about $1,500 an ounce and would have to top $2,000 an ounce when adjusted for inflation to match its value in 1980.

# The end of inflated leverage

An extreme relaxation of lending standards inflated the housing bubble.

Shoddy underwriting on mortgages is the primary cause of the housing crisis. People got caught off-guard by how bad it was.

Millions of home buyers — poor, rich and middle class — were approved to buy homes at prices that had been out-of-reach just a few years earlier. Lenders offered low introductory "teaser" rates on adjustable rate mortgages and approved borrowers based on artificially low mortgage payments, not the higher ones that took effect later.

What else changed:

• **Optional payments on principal** —In 2005, 29% of new mortgages allowed borrowers to pay interest only — not principal — or pay less than the interest due and add the cost to the principal. That was up from 1% in 2001, according to Credit Suisse, an investment bank.

• **No verification of income** —Half of mortgages generated in 2006 required no or minimal documentation of household income, reports Credit Suisse.

• **Tiny down payments** —In 1989, the average down payment for first-time home buyers were 10%, reports the National Association of Realtors. In 2007, it was 2%.

Low down payments and ARMs gave homeowners enormous financial leverage to pay high home prices. Leverage boosts buying power through debt, the same way a 100-pound woman uses a lever to jack up a 3,000-pound car.

Consider a couple with $20,000 cash. In 2006, they easily could get a 5% down mortgage to buy a $400,000 house. Today, a 10% down payment would limit the couple to a $200,000 house.

Easy access to borrowed money reset all housing prices, even those paid by cautious borrowers. People of all income classes moved up a notch, Census Bureau housing data show.

The sale of new homes costing $750,000 or more quadrupled from 2002 to 2006. The construction of inexpensive homes costing $125,000 or less fell by two-thirds. The biggest boom was in the middle. Homes costing $200,000 to $300,000 became affordable to millions of families.

The failed titans of home lending — Countrywide Financial, Indy Mac Bank and Washington Mutual — specialized in high-risk, highly leveraged loans.

The price correction has been severe, rapid and probably permanent, because lending standards have changed. We are not going to see 2006 peak levels for a very, very long time.

## What the Housing Crisis Looks Like

Rick Wallick moved into a new, three-bedroom $200,000 home in Maricopa, Ariz., in October 2005. Today, the home is worth $80,000.

The disabled software engineer stopped making mortgage payments this month. His $70,000 down payment is now worthless. His dream house will be foreclosed on next year.

"We're so far underwater it's not funny," says Wallick, 57, who had to return to his original home in

Oregon to care for a sick family member and tend to his own medical problems. Wallick, one of the hardest-hit victims in one of the states hit hardest by the housing crisis, lost 60% of his home's value in three years.

His story is an extreme example, but home values have fallen so sharply since hitting a historic peak in the spring of 2006 that many Americans are wondering how much more prices can sink.

As painful as the decline has been, history suggests home values still may have a long way to drop and may take decades to return to the heights of 2½ years ago.

"We will never see these prices again in our lifetime, when you adjust for inflation," says Peter Schiff, president of investment firm Euro Pacific Capital of Darien, Conn. "These were lifetime peaks."

The huge increase in home prices — fueled by special financing and low down payments — made it easy to forget that housing values had been remarkably stable for a half-century after World War II, rising at roughly the same pace as income and inflation. Prices soared in most of the country — especially in Arizona, California, Florida and Nevada and metro areas of Washington, D.C., and New York — during a brief period of easy lending, especially from 2002 to 2006. That era's over.

As of 2011, home values nationally have tumbled an average of 30% from their peak. As bad as that is, prices would need to fall as least 10% more to reach their traditional relationship to household income, since 1950. In that scenario, a $300,000 house in 2006 could be worth about $200,000 when real estate prices hit bottom.

# Foreclosures

Goods and services are different than homes. The fragility of our banking system is tied to the value of homes.

The crash in home prices has caused the worst financial crisis since the Great Depression and has wiped out trillions of dollars in home equity. As of 2011, prices are still falling and people fear that the falling prices will never end and that foreclosures and tight credit will send home prices falling to the point that millions of families and thousands of banks will be thrust into insolvency. The government is looking now at doing an additional stimulus package.

We've seen home prices fall before, as seen during the Great Depression and in Texas after the 1980s oil boom, but those drops were a response to other economic forces. This time, the house price collapse was the cause of the nation's economic troubles, not just an effect.

Going back in time, National Association of Realtors chief economist Lawrence Yun predicted home prices will keep falling in 2009 but could return to their 2006 peak in three years, not counting inflation. That didn't exactly happen.

What we saw instead was rapidly falling home prices, similar to the Depression, and as of 2011 are keeping potential buyers and lenders away and fueling even sharper price declines.

Lenders want bigger down payments to protect against the falling value of collateral. Homeowners lose equity, so they can't buy other houses. "Price declines can be a self-reinforcing mechanism," Baker says.

14

An out-of-control price collapse would have dire consequences, Baker says. Even the most conservative banks would find themselves carrying portfolios of toxic mortgage loans.

If housing prices don't stabilize at traditional levels, financial troubles could spread everywhere — to credit cards, car loans and commercial mortgages, Baker says. "The waves of bad debt will just keep coming," he says.

Baker wants the U.S. government to take aggressive steps to help homeowners, not just financial institutions. They support expanding programs that restructure troubled mortgages to prevent a flood of foreclosed homes from coming on the market and driving prices below their traditional level.

An example of how even conservative borrowers can be hurt by price collapse is Rick Wallick. He made a 35% down payment on his house and got a 15-year, fixed-rate mortgage at 5.75% on a home in Arizona. However, the Arizona price collapse caused by speculative buyers wiped him out anyway. Now that he's in Oregon, he's renting out his Arizona house at a loss and can't afford to keep two homes.

Wallick's Arizona house is surrounded by countless foreclosed homes and empty lots. Wallick had no other choice but to tell his lender on the home in Arizona that he wouldn't be making anymore payments. "It may ruin my credit rating, but I can still buy food," he says.

Arizona's real estate mess wiped him out anyway. Now that he's in Oregon, he's renting out his Arizona house at a loss and can't afford to keep two homes.

Wallick's Arizona house is surrounded by countless foreclosed homes and empty lots. He told his mortgage company that his December payment will be his last. "It may ruin my credit rating, but I can still buy food," he says.

Shelley McComb used a no-money-down, interest-only ARM to pay $199,000 in December 2006 for a new three-bedroom home near Birmingham, Ala. The house's assessed value briefly rose to $225,000.

Now, she needs to move to Atlanta where her husband got a promotion. The McCombs put their home up for sale in March. After getting no offers, they dropped their price to $179,000. They'd settle for $160,000.

Shelley McComb, 30, who manages a doggie day care center, says, "I wish we'd rented."

## *Key Points from this Chapter*

- Housing prices follow income. This is why it's going to be so difficult for prices to come back to where they were in 2006. It was a bubble and people were over buying because of easy credit that will not be coming back.

- The economy in the U.S. will continue to cause fear in people and they will be cautious about buying stocks. This will affect economic growth.

- The government needs to spend more money on services, which right now it can't afford. The world is not comfortable with countries overspending as we saw with Greece in 2010. Many people will have less government income.

- Large down payments required by banks will cause fewer people to purchase homes as we have traditionally seen.

# THE PRESENT

# Chapter 3:

# Accepting What is the New Economy

The music is going to stop eventually and the investors are going to realize that the word "recovery" is tougher than we think. The economy can never recover in our lives to the pace and frenzy of the bubble years – and that's good. The question will then be: What will the new economy look like?

One important detail about the new economy is the value of US stocks will be very different – meaning not as valued – as they are now. Companies will make money, especially the ones taking advantage of the growing economies throughout the world. But investors are likely to place lower values on them regardless. That's what happens in a bear market; the price-to-earnings ratio falls. Earnings do not necessarily go down; but the multiple investors are willing to pay for each dollar of earnings does.

In good economies, investors are willing to pay 20 or 30 times for each dollar of earnings. But when they are gloomy and in a struggling economy, they're unwilling to pay anything more than 10 or even 5 times for each dollar of earnings.

Americans, and to a lesser extent people living in other developed economies, are going to feel increasingly negative as the years go by. For one thing, their economies are likely to underperform their competitors in the emerging world. But I'm going to focus on another reason today: their government financing systems are fundamentally dishonest and bankrupt. To make a long story short, their economies have been living on borrowed money and borrowed time. The moment for settling up is approaching. It is going to be painful, gloomy and depressing. All asset classes – save maybe cash and gold – are likely to fall.

## Today's Environment

A lot of property owners find themselves caught in a bad position, because banks won't lend more than the real estate is worth. Property values have declined significantly since the bubble burst. Many property owners owe more on their homes than they are currently worth. With stricter lending practices adopted by banks, homeowners are unable to refinance their properties to 30 fixed rates because they are under water with no residual remaining.

The investing strategies practiced just a few years ago (during the boom years) are now terribly inadequate for succeeding in today's distressed real estate market. Investors need to think and act differently if they want to survive this down cycle and profit when the economy eventually rebounds.

While fully recognizing the mistakes of the past and providing sound advice for taking advantage of future opportunities, this book explains how to successfully invest in today's distressed market. Recent developments have crushed many real estate speculators, but they have also created profitable new opportunities for individuals willing to serve as the next generation of contrarian investors – a generation that will undoubtedly make their fortunes by buying when everyone else is desperately selling. This book offers effective strategies for taking advantage of this new era of investing. Though most of yesterday's most favored strategies no longer work, today's savvy real estate investors can still find great opportunities for growth and profit – if, of course, they acknowledge how recent events are altering the real estate landscape and if they determine how to take full advantage of the situation.

Investors must return to the sound fundamentals that have worked for centuries. It's back to "blocking and tackling" and doing what has consistently worked in the past – buying on cash flow and disregarding the notion of automatic price appreciation. Increases in value during this tough cycle will be dependent on your property's Net Operating Income. You can't do much about the economy, so you must add value. Buying at distressed and greatly depreciated prices is a good start. If you're going to make money in real estate during these challenging times – you'll have to earn it the hard way.

## What's to Come Next?

"This economic crisis doesn't represent a cycle. It represents a reset," Jeff Immelt, the CEO of General Electric, said. "It's an emotional, social, economic reset." And the biggest impact of this "reset" will be greater government involvement in the economy, and in the affairs of business, for better or worse. "People who understand that will prosper," Immelt said. "Those who don't will be left behind."

As this reset applies to real estate, property values will go lower and as deleveraging takes place, debt-to-equity ratios will become more manageable. Only people with great credit will have access to loans and they will be required to use very large down payments.

Real estate investors should expect a wave of foreclosures on over-leveraged properties to continue during this year. That being said, I anticipate single-family homes and rental apartments to be on the forefront of a recovery. A reduction in construction will limit supply while demand rises because of immigration, retiring baby boomers, and 80 million echo boomers leaving college to enter the workforce (more on that later in the book). Office and retail will falter from 2011 to 2012, because property owners won't be able to get money for capital improvements to keep tenants. But, once again, tremendous financial opportunity can always be found during distressed cycles.

In the post-crisis landscape, success in real estate will be defined by an unwavering concentration on the fundamentals – valuing properties based on their existing merits coupled with a realistic approach to determining both the current and future financial potential of a given asset.

## *Key Points from this Chapter*

- There are opportunities with the aging population as their needs change in housing along with the Echo boomers leaving college.
- The greatest increase in overall population growth since the 1950 will give incredible opportunity to provide affordable housing.
- The country – and the world – is deleveraging and not carrying so much debt.
- Lending will be tighter to get and reserved for those with large down payments and great credit. This is both on the commercial and residential side.

# Chapter 4:  A Buyer's Market

When a real estate market goes down, we call it a buyer's market.  A buyer's market is characterized by having more sellers than buyers, and as a result of supply and demand – prices go down.

Prior to 2007, real estate was overvalued and up for and enormous price correction.  Buyers are now able to buy residential and commercial real estate at significant discounts.  Experts estimate that commercial real estate operating revenue is down by 30 to 40 percent; therefore, buyers are well positioned to negotiate aggressively on acquisitions.  With values still falling, there has never been a better time for investors to be acquiring real estate.

When a market crashes, prices don't go to a "fair" price.  Instead, they go past historical average levels to a point of being seriously undervalued (the bottom's bottom).  Typically on the upside of a real estate cycle, developers tent to over build, so there's excess inventory coming onto the market. However, consumers lose confidence in the economy after a bubble bursts. Lenders grow leery of exposing themselves to more risk, thereby making it more difficult to secure a mortgage, which reduces demand even further.

## Residential Market

In the residential arena, Realtors consider a balanced market to be one in which homes take an average of six months to sell. This is tracked by calculating the days on market (DOM) for every home listed and sold. If the average DOM rises above six months, then the market is becoming more favorable to buyers. If it falls below that threshold, it is becoming a seller's market. In a buyer's market, there are essentially too many homes for sale for the number of buyers, so inventory increases, homes take longer to sell, and sellers become more motivated and eventually decrease their asking prices.

For example, real estate in Naples, Florida, was considered the most overvalued in the country in 2006. Today, real estate in Naples sells at a 30-plus percent average discount, and the median home price is just $165,500, down from a high of nearly $400,000, according to HIS Global Insight.

## Commercial Market

Commercial real estate is valued on one figure called the cap rate. It assumes that the property is only worth what the rents less the expenses are. However there is some adjustments made for the age and condition. There are different asset classes in commercial real estate (multifamily, retail, office, industrial), and those classes will be selling below, at, or above the average historical rate. If cap rates are far below the average (as we experienced during that past decade in a compressed cap-rate environment), it's a seller's market. If cap rates are higher than the average, it's a buyer's market. Cap rates historically have run between 8% for top-tier properties to 12% for low-tier properties.

For example, in a buyer's market you would pay a higher cap rate. Historically, the average cap rate for multifamily properties is approximately 8 percent. If you're buying at a 12 percent cap rate, it would indicate you are paying less for the income. Many first-time buyers needed a significant price correction to be able to afford commercial real estate properties. And experienced investors needed a reset in values in order to justify new acquisitions. Ultimately, investors are more likely to maximize their returns if they are acquiring during a buyer's market and in disposition mode during a seller's market.

## *Key Points from this Chapter*

- Markets can be traced over history to determine a reasonable price to purchase.
- A buyer's market is when it's taking a long time to sell property – normally more than six months.
- Watch for markets that have been over-sold and are below their historical levels, based on affordability (percent of income to home value) and historical prices.

# Chapter 5:  Foreclosed Properties

When we refer to distressed properties, what we are talking about is a property that is either in foreclosure – or even has been foreclosed on and is owned by the bank – or a property that has been run down physically. Distressed properties commonly have and owner or a lender holding the note on the property that is motivated to sell.  This is one of the great opportunities for investors to buy a property at a significant discount to the fair market value.

For a distressed seller, obtaining the highest price possible isn't necessarily the goal.  Instead, disposing of the real estate in a timely manner is of greater importance. Therefore, selling at a price below market value is the norm and not the exception with most distressed situations. The discount obtained in acquiring distressed real estate provides additional equity for the new buyer.

There are two types of distressed properties:
- Physically distressed real estate: The property has a problem and needs to be fixed. Perhaps, it's in poor physical condition or needs capital improvements. For example, the real estate may be run down or dilapidated.
- Financially distressed real estate: This refers to the financial condition or state of the property. For example, the owner might not be able to maintain the mortgage payments because the property has been mismanaged, thus resulting in a higher than anticipated vacancy rate that fails to generate sufficient income for the owner to meet the monthly debt service. The property could also be in some state of foreclosure or at risk of foreclosure. The lender might agree to short sale or sell the asset as an REO (real estate owned). The lender might also be willing to sell the note at a discount of the balance owed on the mortgage, and the new buyer would assume responsibility for the foreclosure proceedings to take control of the real estate. Perhaps the owner is distressed because of divorce, death, or poor health. Or, perhaps, the property owner's loan might be maturing and he or she is unable to refinance the existing debt because of lack of equity.

All these scenarios depict circumstances in which investors have the possibility to acquire real estate at significant discounts. During the new economy, investors are buying properties at bargain-basement prices from owners and lenders who are struggling. The volume of real estate transaction in so-called distressed properties will ultimately stabilize the market. But, until then, vulture funds and other savvy investors will continue to circle the skies looking for distressed bargains to prey upon.

## RTC Crisis versus the New Economy

The mortgage industry suffered a major setback in 1989, the year of the savings and loan crisis. Billions of dollars in savings were lost, and taxpayers had to foot the bill for the huge bailout that was the result of the Financial Institutions Reform, Recovery and Enforcement Act of 1989 (FIRREA). An outgrowth of FIRREA was the Resolution Trust Corp. (RTC), a quasi-public agency that closed 747 thrifts and S&Ls, whose primary activity was mortgage loans, in six years. $90 billion in losses were incurred, and the amount paid for by taxpayers.

FIRREA created new regulations that required thrifts to have more capital to back up deposits; and it also allowed the government to take over the thrifts that did not meet the new requirements. Midsize thrifts were required to hold 70 percent of their portfolios in residential real estate mortgages, and small thrifts were restricted in the size of loans they could make, with the biggest loan possible being 10 percent of capital. FIRREA also opened up the Federal Home Loan Bank to commercial banks, giving them the same access to wholesale funds that were previously available only to thrifts. The legislation changed the S&L landscape forever, and many thrifts did not survive because they were unable to meet the stringent requirements, or unable to compete against larger, commercial banks. While risky ventures and in some cases, fraud were to blame for the failure of thrifts, many still blame the deregulation and FIRREA for making it impossible for thrifts to continue competing. In the midst of the crisis, many observers predicted that S&Ls would cease to exist entirely; and although today that has not happened, there are decidedly fewer of them, primarily among smaller communities. According to the Milken Institute, an independent economic think tank, fraud was a factor in only 10 percent of the S&L failures.

Nearly a trillion dollars of assets were seized from failed S&Ls, and the RTC was brought into being to dispose of them at fire-sale pricesýcreating opportunities for real estate entrepreneurs, but at the same time, being the spark that ignited the recession of the 1990s.

There have been nearly endless buying opportunities in the residential sector since the housing collapse in 2007. The bid-ask spread (the difference between what investors were willing to pay and the amount of lenders were willing to sell) narrowed in 2008, and distressed opportunities have become the primary driving force of transactions ever since.

In vast contrast to the residential sector, there has not been as much activity as originally anticipated with distressed commercial assets. Federal regulators have not forced banks to mark to market their bad loans and liquidate their inventory of nonperforming assets. Lenders are savvy to what occurred during the RTC days and want to avoid massive losses. Many lenders prefer to stay the course and sell when the market rebounds. Until the regulators become more forceful, it's unlikely that large scale deleveraging will occur. That being said, I'm confident we'll ultimately have more deals being consummated on commercial properties (retail, office, industrial, and multifamily). Lenders will eventually realize the cost of extending loans that are underwater and will sell to the highest bidder, especially if the FDIC forces them to do so. Vulture funds have formed to buy all distressed real estate assets, and war chests are being consolidated for a buying spree that many anticipate could last from 2011 through 2015.

## Advantages of Buying a Distressed Property

There are a number of advantages to buying a distressed property:

- A highly motivated seller – either a bank in the case of and REO/foreclosure or owners who are in financial trouble and very interested in getting out of a mortgage they can no longer afford.
- Less emotion from the seller's perspective because the lender considers it a line-item loss to sell for a discount and is interested in getting properties sold and off the liability side of the lender's balance sheet.
- Many foreclosed properties can be purchased for only a percentage of what they would have commanded at the height of the market and at a discount of the current market value.

# Disadvantages of Buying a Distressed Property

Disadvantages of buying a distressed property include:
- Although there are bargains to be had, they don't come easily. Great deals are hard won, and there's always competition that can inevitably lead to higher prices.
- There tends to be more legal work required to complete a distressed transaction.
- The time required for short sales or foreclosures often takes longer than traditional transactions.
- Distressed properties can be in tough condition. Owners who know they are going to lose the capital they originally invested are unlikely to maintain the property as they did before, and, in fact, they might even purposely damage it.

Distressed real estate represents a tremendous opportunity for all investors. Most important, it's an opportunity to acquire real estate assets at steep discounts. And given the record number of foreclosures and the tightening credit market, it will remain a buyer's market for distressed assets for the next several years. Remain optimistic and creative during this cycle. This could be the best time to acquire real estate in our lifetime. Despite what the pundits might say about the demise of real estate and the recession's impact on the industry, opportunities abound, and fortunes will be made as astute investors purchase distressed properties now and either hold them long-term for their cash flow or resell them when the market rebounds.

## *Key Points from this Chapter*

- Distressed real estate represents a tremendous opportunity for all investors.
- Vulture funds have formed to buy all distressed real estate assets, and war chests are being consolidated for a buying spree that many anticipate could last from 2011 through 2013.
- Obtaining the highest possible price isn't necessarily the goal of a distressed seller. Rather, disposing of the property in a timely manner is of greater importance.

# Chapter 6: Reinventing Yourself in the New Economy

Even the most seasoned investors could not have foreseen the real estate crash of 2007. There was a time during that decade that we all thought that real estate prices would go up as sure as the sun would rise. But those days are gone.

Real estate had its best years in the history of our nation during that run up. Everyone that got in the game of buying, fixing-up, and selling the property made money – a lot of money. The lending standards made it possible for far too many people to be involved in the business and in the process drove prices to unrealistic levels. There was a sense of euphoria that enticed the vast majority of investors to shun the time-tested financial models used to value income producing real estate. Instead, paying a premium was considered logical and appropriate, assuming, of course, that values would continue to soar. Very few investors envisioned a real estate market in decline.

There was a time, up until the real estate boom, that investors could buy apartment buildings at a decent price, that would give them a return on their investment. The model used to value rental properties was fairly conservative, but was in no way just a random purchase like the condo converters that came to the game later. The properties had to generate cash after all their expenses that was a good return. Fortunately, many investors avoided the get-rich quick schemes that trapped most condo converters at the time- especially those who were late to the game. During the boom most apartment buildings were acquired at numbers that could not support the individual units as condos. In other words, the sum of the individual parts was worth more than the entire asst as a whole. But if the market tumbled before exiting, the owner would need to carry a very expensive piece of real estate that could potentially "bleed" him dry.

By 2005, a new way to make money in apartments came about in converting them to condos. In large cities, investors were converting luxury hotels into condos, but either way, conversions were extremely profitable. If you owned apartments, the market was ripe to sell during that severely compressed, cap-rate environment. Buildings that were originally purchased at 9 percent cap rates were receiving offers in the 3 to 4 percent range. Smart owners simply couldn't justify the risk/reward analysis of holding their properties. The logic was, "Pigs get fat and hogs get slaughtered."

For several years, from 2005 to 2009, you couldn't buy apartments better than a 5 percent cap rate. That meant even if you put 25 percent down payment, you couldn't generate cash flow after debt service.

I had been developing subdivisions and entitling properties my business partner and I had purchased. Some properties we owned out-right, but others had debt. By 2008, we had not been able to get financing to develop the curb and gutter of the subdivision in our quest to create value and profit. We had created a situation that was bleeding us dry. We learned the real world lesson of cash-flow in real estate, but it was too late. The world was in a world-wide, banking crisis. We, like every other real estate developer, were in serious trouble.

Most successful entrepreneurs realize that reinventing themselves and their businesses is a healthy process that can pay huge dividends if executed properly. If what you had been doing in the past no longer works, you need to change gears, develop a new way of thinking, and change your business model to meet the demands of a new environment.

I figured out that banks were not going to be lending money to develop ground. We started to see banks taking back fully developed subdivisions where all that was left was to complete the construction. The banks in most cases were selling the developed lots below what the cost was for the materials and the ground was, in essence, free.

We began meeting with investors and put together a business plan where we could lower prices and sell off the remaining foreclosed lots banks were offering at a discount. The plan included finishing both townhome and single-family subdivisions, where we were also building homes with experienced builders.

In fact, our first significant project was a large townhome project the developer was foreclosed on, because the property values had come down and the bank was requiring a large amount of money from him to bring the loan to value in line with their lending requirements. The developer ended up giving the bank the property back. Fortunately, we were the first in line to buy the property. The bank had to take some time to figure out what they were going to do with the property and during that time we met with them and showed them what we would make by developing the property out. The opportunity was for us to raise cash from investors, since there was no bank that would loan on any property at the time. We showed that we would be below market and even below the price of existing short sales and foreclosure. The investors look like they are going to profit greatly and sales, although they have been slow, are doing well.

We had changed our business model from owning properties to charging consulting fees for investors and helping them profit from distressed properties. Through sheer will and determination, we were able to keep our attitudes positive and find like-minded investors willing to see the opportunities and profit. We had created a profit center in the middle of what seemed like a financial desert.

Joe Beall is a Las Vegas real estate broker. He had done quite well for himself during the boom years, but he quickly realized (after barely surviving a financially disastrous 2007) that he needed to change his business model. He was determined to survive the downturn and realized that the market's appetite for real estate speculation had gone from boom to bust. Also, he understood the importance of changing his model to prosper in a depleted real estate economy.

He immediately stopped trying to sell preconstruction condominiums and started a vigorous campaign to partner with lender-processing service companies. These firms provide automated loan processing, risk management, and other support services that completed the process from loan making to payoff. He realized that these service providers were the banks' gatekeepers in liquidating distressed properties. If he could find a way to partner with these companies, he would position himself as the "go-to" broker for moving a significant amount of real estate at discounted prices. And sales of distressed real estate, in his opinion, were where the future opportunity existed. He would change his model of selling fewer properties at high prices to selling significantly more properties at discounted prices. Beall explained the boom years as days filled by writing up offers and sending them out to property owners. His buyers would typically bid more than the asking price on all of his transactions. There were very few listings available, so he concentrated on the buy side. He closed 17 deals with one client in November 2005. His buyers would acquire and then flip, so he had multiple transactions with each client. During the apex of euphoria (2004 to 2005), one of his clients earned a net profit of approximately $3.5 million on more than 100 transactions.

Beall said, "My savvy clients started dumping everything in early 2006. They wanted out immediately." By the first quarter of 2007, the market had completely changed. His customers were inquiring about short sales, so he bought every book on the subject and attended distressed real estate seminars in an effort to learn as much as possible.

He called local bank representatives every day for four months before he received his first REO listing. By late 2007, he was doing 7 – 10 short sales a month and was 100 percent dedicated to distressed real estate. He even expanded his services to help banks maintain their properties until they could be sold. He hired cleanup crews, locksmiths, maintenance personnel, and other specialists to help banks with their new real estate responsibilities.

Beall now claims that he works harder than ever before, but the money is still very good. The year 2010 was extremely busy. He was inundated with calls from buyers wanting to acquire distressed real estate. All his transactions are short sales. Thankfully, the banks are finally cooperating.

He says that he expects short sales to remain his "bread and butter" business through 2011 and 2012. In fact, a typical month in 2010 yielded 17 transactions, and he's just as busy now as he was during the boom – he earned a high six-figure income in 2010.

A friend of mine is a real estate attorney for a well respected law firm in Utah. At one time, he primarily worked on closings and had and extremely busy practice until 2006. When the number of closings started to slide, he realized that it was time to change the way he did business. Otherwise, he wouldn't have survived for much longer.

He came to the conclusion that the deep market fissures in the housing market would last for several more years, so he convinced his law firm to reposition him as the head legal counsel for its REO department. I'm glad to report that, as of late 2010, he was closing on average 90 – 100 deals each month and making three times his previous salary.

The moral of the story is that you shouldn't expect the same spectacular results every year if you don't consider modifying your business strategy to adapt to the changing times. Whatever you had been doing from 2000 to 2007 will likely no longer work. This is a new economy, and the sooner you realize it the better off you'll be. The only way to achieve long-term success in real estate (or any other industry, of that matter) is to embrace a periodic reinvention and or modification of what you do and how you do it and to accept change as necessary to your survival. You must determine where the new opportunities exist and how to leverage your skills and expertise to take your piece of the distressed American pie. It's time to sink or swim – to flounder or flourish. Welcome to the new economy.

## *Key Points from this Chapter*

- You shouldn't expect the same spectacular results every year if you don't consider modifying your business strategy to adapt to the changing times.
- If what you had been doing in the past no longer works, you need to change gears, develop a new way of thinking, and change your business model to meet the demands of a new environment.
- Many people are making more money after the boom than in the run-up years.

# THE OPPORTUNITY

# Chapter 7: The Gold Rush of 1849

The American dream started with the pilgrims working hard their whole life, sacrificing for a better day. They were content to slowly accumulate modest fortunes over a lifetime of hard work. Benjamin Franklin wrote "Who is rich? He that is content. Who is that? Nobody." The culture was aware of overspending and not being content.

The American dream, however, was suddenly shattered in 1849 with the discovery of gold in California. Significant wealth creation – earned virtually overnight by sheer will, determination, and a fair amount of good luck in the gold mines of Northern California – ruled the day. Instant gratification became the new mantra in America.

Yes, the notion of getting rich quickly went all the way back to the 49ers of the mid-nineteenth century and as recently seen in the Internet entrepreneurs of the 90s.

But it's not just Americans that love the get-rich-quick ideas. When gold was discovered in Northern California, millions of Americans, Europeans, and Asians immediately migrated to the area. San Francisco became the geographical focal point for anyone who aspired to overnight fame and fortune. The city quickly grew and soon became a rival of New York in terms of wealth, prestige, and commerce. A small number of prospectors who searched for gold in California's rivers and mines found the fortune they were hoping for. Unfortunately, however, the vast majority of 49ers left California as poor (if not poorer) as when they had arrived. By vast contrast, significantly more fortunes were made from entrepreneurs who provided goods and service to the millions of miners and other migrants who had relocated to the area.

This is the interesting fact: Merchants, in fact, made more than miners during and after the gold rush of 1849. Allow me to repeat myself: "Merchants made more money than miners during and after the gold rush of 1849." The profundity of this statement and how it applies to you requires further explanation.

Most people, especially those arriving late to California, didn't get rich and most made little to nothing. Overall, few gold seekers made any money in search of gold.

Other businesspeople, through good fortune and hard work, reaped great fortunes in retail, entertainment, lodging, and transportation. In other words, fortunes were made in sectors that had nothing to do with gold but everything to do with savvy entrepreneurs who realized a good business opportunity and seized the moment. Many service-oriented businesses were highly profitable because of the influx of people to Northern California. After all, the gold seekers left everything behind from where they came but needed to sustain themselves while they were in California.

Samuel Brannan was the wealthiest man in California during the gold rush according to historical records. He was a successful shopkeeper who opened the first supply stores near the Northern California gold fields. He supplied the gold seekers with basic supplies and made a fortune doing it.

Levi Strauss was another such fortune maker with great vision and an eye for future opportunities. Arriving I California in the 1850s, Strauss opened a dry goods wholesale business. Strauss sold a variety of goods to the supply stores throughout California. However, one product eventually became one of the most enduring fixtures in American culture: Levi's jeans. Levi Strauss initially introduced the durable pants to miners in the gold mines, but they remained popular long after the gold rush ended. In fact, more than 150 years later, Levi Strauss & Co. has become one of the largest apparel marketers in the world with sales in more than 100 countries.

OK (take a deep breath), how is this relevant to you and real estate investing in this new economy? Well, there have been many booms and busts during recorded history:

- In the 1630's, the tulip bulb mania in Holland was followed by a sudden collapse in prices. This was thought to be the first speculative bubble in recorded history.

- In the 1840s and 1850s, the California gold rush (as previously described) was followed by a tumultuous economic collapse in Northern California that transformed once-prosperous mining towns into ghost towns.
- The Roaring '20s were followed by the Great Depression and the collapse of the stock market that started in 1929.
- In the late 1990s, the dot-com bubble was followed by the Internet implosion.
- And by the early twenty-first century, the boom in U.S. real estate was followed by the subprime mortgage crisis, global economic meltdown, and the Great Recession.

I have been an active participant, beneficiary, and avid student of the past two bubbles. But I think it would be helpful to reflect on the successes of the 1840s to better understand how some entrepreneurs developed unique and highly profitable businesses in a changing market.

When news of the California Gold Rush made its way east, Levi Strauss decided to emigrate to San Francisco to make his fortune: not by panning gold, but by selling supplies to the throngs of miners who arrived daily in the big city to outfit themselves before heading off to the gold fields. He began selling canvas to use for tents. Soon he realized that prospectors needed pants that were sufficiently durable to withstand the hard physical labor required from people who worked in mines all day. Strauss decided to use the canvas for overalls for the miners. When the gold rush was over, Strauss didn't shut down his company. Instead, he re-designed the overalls into blue jeans – a product that became wildly popular to a much larger market.

When Levi Strauss migrated from New York to San Francisco, he knew that his fortune wouldn't be made in the gold mines. In other words, he didn't follow the herd. Instead, he remained dedicated to supplying miners with everyday products that they needed. Levi Strauss made his great fortune after the gold rush had subsided by selling millions of his trademark blue jeans to miners and non-miners alike. By altering his product, he was able to broaden his customer base. That's a priceless lesson for today's economy.

## Fortunes Made in Ancillary Businesses

Following the masses in their pursuit of great fortune doesn't always result in the most profitable outcome. During the gold rush, the most obvious decision made by wealth seekers was to search for gold. During the Internet boom, investors bought tech stocks or developed Internet companies. During the real estate boom, they acquired properties. More often than not, however, the business models that lead to the real pot of gold are not so obvious. People with great ingenuity and creativity often develop the very best money making ideas. After all, Levi Strauss didn't pursue the most obvious path (at that time) to great wealth. He wasn't a gold seeker. Rather, he offered a unique product that was widely adopted even after the frenzy subsided.

Lawyers are now making a fortune conducting closing for short sale transactions. Bankruptcy specialists are experiencing an unprecedented boom in this Great Recession. Receivers are turning a very nice profit managing distressed properties during these tough times. Real estate brokers who specialize in foreclosed real estate are doing extremely well during the busted economy. Capitalists are buying real estate at unheard of prices. There are a host of entrepreneurs who now service the distressed real estate sector and are more profitable now than they were during the run-up in real estate values.

## Modifying Your Strategy after the Boom

Successful business owners must have the foresight to change gears before, during, and after a boom in order to make and/or sustain their fortune. Opportunities abound, regardless of the times. An excellent example of this comes from a friend of mine who founded a business to connect "bottom-fishing" real estate investors with distressed condo deals.

Another friend of mine created a web based lead generation company for real estate companies that is affordable and helps agents sell more homes. He was a manager for a real estate company in the boom, when having an Internet presence wasn't necessary. He knew what the agents and owners wanted and also knew how to sell it to people in management. He prepared the whole company to serve agents and it became a valuable recruiting tool for the real estate company he was working for at the time. He figured out how to show owners that the site – Blueroof.com – wouldn't even be a cost, once they figured in how many top agents it would attract and help. He's making more money now than he did as a manager ten-fold. So are the real estate companies.

My business partner and I have re-created ourselves. By leveraging our banking contacts and ability to source distressed real estate, we are brokering multimillion deals for several investment groups from the Western United States. We find distressed projects, conduct the due diligence, assemble the investment team, and manage the property back to health. Our investors supply the capital needed to acquire the assets and my partner and I earn an equity stake and transaction fees for each deal. We also serve as general partner in charge of the day-to-day operations. If you get knocked down, you must find a way to get back up. In the past two years, we've double our investors money in the midst of the worst market in history.

Ideas for viable businesses during challenging economic times aren't always so obvious. Sometimes you'll stumble upon a good concept, and other times you'll methodically develop one out of necessity. Always remember that there are just as many, if not more, profitable opportunities to pursue during the doom-and-gloom years associated with a bust as there are during the go-go days associated with the boom. If you were successful during the boom, then you can be equally successful during the bust. The gold rush gave Levi Strauss his big opportunity, but the period following that boom gave him his fortune. Pay close attention to your ever-changing business environment and be willing to adopt new strategies to profit in the downturn.

## *Key Points from this Chapter*

- Always remember that there are just as many, if not more, profitable opportunities to pursue during the doom-and-gloom years associated with a bust as there are during the go-go days associated with the boom.
- Following the masses in their pursuit of great fortune doesn't always result in the most profitable outcome.
- Significantly more fortunes were made from entrepreneurs who provided goods and service to the millions of miners and other migrants.
- Successful business owners must have the foresight to change gears before, during, and after a boom in order to make and/or sustain their fortune.

# Chapter 8: Who Makes the Big Money

The real estate building business is one of the few areas that a person can enter with little expertise and become wealthy in a short time. With the right financial backing, a little business savvy, and careful attention to detail, you too can earn whatever you want to earn.

# Background

Since most people learn this development business in the school of "hard-knocks", you may be wondering what it takes to learn the business. It is true that good developers must multi-task without letting go of the overall project goal. Developing property with any degree of success relies on interaction well with key players. The steps taken by a typical developer involve working through regulatory channels, the political arena, and gaining neighborhood approval. It requires good negotiating skills and luck. Self-knowledge and creativity are both keys to the success of a real estate development project. In addition, there are many steps from the conception of the project to the final stages that involve contracts with a myriad of people, including buyers, sellers, lenders, contractors, and architects – so that people skills are high on the list of requirements.

A real estate developer can loosely be defined as a person, partnership, or other entity who has an idea for development and subsequently gathers the seed capital to begin the project, purchases a piece of land or a building, and creates the necessary steps for the project to make a profit. As you delve into your first few projects, you may find that you possess a talent for one part or another. You might begin to specialize in particular area, or you may search for partners to round out the total process with you.

A developer can also be defined as someone who purchases an existing property and renovates it or revamps it for a different use. Often these properties where the use has become obsolete through changes in the market, changes in the neighborhood, or simply due to lack of maintenance and updates. Some areas of the country have a tremendous amount of property revitalization. The fact is that the majority of owners as well as tenants have no idea what a property could look like with a renovation or cosmetic upgrades. If you are able to visualize updates to an existing property and you can keep the project cost effective, you may be able to put your ideas into action.

Real estate development projects are all different because there are so many niches, such as developing raw land or renovating existing buildings. You may have a property in mind where you want to build posh upscale homes, or you may want to create a minimalist office building from the ground up. You may choose to sell your improved parcels to others, or lease and manage them yourself, or put any other combination of all the above ideas into play. With development, you can invent your own job from an array of endless possibilities.

Whether developers are interested in land, multifamily residential, office, industrial, or retail development, or mixed use properties, there are always numerous opportunities. Most developers choose to specialize in a particular segment of these general areas; for example, building strip malls will differ from building regional malls.

Developers you know may differ widely in their skills, their ego, and the level of visibility that they prefer. Developers may choose to concentrate on one type of property or several. They may work in small niche, regionally or nationally. One who has skills in construction may choose to act as general contractor as well, and another whose background is in finance may choose to hire out that portion of their project. Some choose to work alone, and some choose to work in partnership with others. All developers have a few things in common, though; they must have access to land and capital, and they must have- or develop- skills for management and entrepreneurship.

## Education

There are many programs leading to bachelor's degrees, MBA's, and certifications in various aspects of real estate. Columbia Business School, for example, offers an MBA in real estate that combines the hands-on experience of an internship with courses in finance and negotiations. Georgia State University's degrees range from certificate in real estate to an undergraduate degree, an MBA, and MSRE, and a PhD in real estate. A partial listing of college programs in real estate development is given at the end of this chapter. However, new programs are cropping up all the time, so a person who is interested in developing the educational end of their experience could start with local colleges and universities to find classes. Many courses are also offered online, or with low residency so that you can do some course work at home and spend minimal time on campus to fulfill your requirements. These schools work hard at fine tuning their programs to offer a complete education program that will fit the student for the job.

About half of the people in the business get a formal degree and the other half teach themselves. In fact, until the 1970's, there were really no programs that offered a college-level concentration in real estate. Some professionals say that about 70 percent of what a developer needs to know has to be learned in the field. If you are not trained in the business, do not be intimidated by others who are. Education is only one of many tools that can prepare you for the business.

Real estate development is not for amateurs, yet it can be accomplished successfully by people from all walks of life. According to the Urban Land Institute, the average developer may have a background in accounting, business, real estate, construction, lending, project management, or be a student. Your background alone does not determine the likelihood of your success. Real estate developers create the very basis of urban life as we know it. Their dreams become a reality that changes our landscape for years to come.

Many developers begin by working as an apprentice for someone else to gain knowledge of the field before striking out on their own. If this is your plan, you should be aware from the outset that some employers will want you to have an advanced degree, even an MBA or equivalent, and corporate experience. If you are considering working for someone else, experts agree that you can go into any part of the process that fits you and your capabilities, because you can move from one area to another easily. It does not seem to matter whether you start in private or public company; you can learn well in either.

There are more than five million professionals in the real estate field. A great many professional developers have worked their way up the ladder without benefit of these tools, so do not give up on the dream without exploring all of the options available to you

My personal background is a Bachelor's Degree from the University of Utah. I sold real estate while I was in college and then I started a title insurance company after I graduated. I ran the title insurance company with two business partners for nearly 20 years. During the time at the title company, I learned about working with government agencies, title laws that affect properties, liens that affect new construction, financing laws, and marketing, overseeing different groups of people working on the same project, closing costs, real estate finance, leasing concepts, accounting and living by a budget. Every concept of real estate development was covered in my 20 years of insuring real estate transactions. What I didn't learn, which I ended up paying for personally, were the things nobody likes to talk about: Mistakes that are unforeseen because of a real estate bubble. Those lessons cost me millions of dollars of my own money and are probably the lessons that make my experience so valuable. I don't think it's possible to be in the real estate development business and not have losses. It's the nature of the development business.

## Traits of a Developer

A developer is someone who is very active in the process. People who invest but do not participate are investors; people who find tenants or buyers and receive commission are brokers. Development is different from being a broker because of the personal risk involved. In developing, you have total control, yet no control at all; you risk everything, and you may gain more than would ever be possible in any of the other connected roles; and perhaps more than any other career, you rely a great deal on instinct.

Although most of the skills you will need can be learned through reading, taking classes, or by learning on the job, there are a few traits you must have from the beginning, and I would like to mention those here. If you do not have them, they can be acquired.

- **Being a developer means you have a drive to succeed**
  You are excited about your work and it shows. You get a high from the challenge of the game itself. You thrive on risk, and you push to be the best that you can be on every level.

- **Being a developer requires a great deal of flexibility**
  Developers have to shift strategies quickly. They make changes simply to cause the project to meet public approval. They hire and fire employees, renegotiate financing, and contract with buyers or tenants. Deadlines will move forward and back, or simply become unattainable due to circumstances beyond all control.

- **Being a developer means having or acquiring skill in marketing, supervision, finance, and risk management**
  At any point in the process, a developer may be acting as creator, promoter, negotiator, or investor. They must market to tenants, buyers, and the public. They supervise the entire design and construction team. They work with investors and lenders. They cope with the internal pressures associated with high risk on a daily basis.

- **Great developers have a tried and proven process**

  To be successful in real estate development you have to have a methodical process where you work the details and follow a plan. If you find details that derail you, developers have the intestinal fortitude and discipline to walk away from a transaction.

- **Being a developer means having tenacity**

  It is a complex business requiring a complex entrepreneur at its helm. Developers have to assemble the talents, manage individuals, make things happen, withstand intense pressure and uncertainty, lead, coordinate, and give their team a clear vision. A developer must be able to sell his idea to his team and to the public. He must have the common sense to know to let go when the risk is too great and outweighs the benefits.

Over and over, real estate developers, as I've thought about my own seasoning I think you must be willing to continue to learn. Jim Anderson with Elliott Bearnt & Knox LLP, said, "The most important personality trait is to accept that you are not perfect and then be open to learning. Developers should admit that it is a learning process. In fact, the most successful developers that I have worked with are the ones who are content to be a generalist, and then rely on experts to do the detail work."

It is a detail business. A friend of mine told me when I got into this business that he could retire on the money he lost to lazy due-diligence. Be willing to triple check every detail, otherwise you can easily work for several years on a project and make no money because of a few small mistakes. Ultimately, you are responsible for zoning changes, even if they take place as a result of public pressure, skipped or overlooked tests, undiscovered land issues, and false promises that may arise out of your transaction.

## Who Makes the Big Money?

Did you know that 46 out of the world's 691 billionaires made their fortunes in the real estate industry? Well, according to Forbes magazine's 2010 annual list of "The World's Richest People," this elite group has quite a bit in common between their habits, lifestyles, and business styles. Here are some unifying qualities shared by America's richest real estate moguls.

**1. Go commercial.** Billionaires who make their fortunes in real estate don't do it in residential. They are moguls with an empire of owned and operated office buildings, shopping centers, apartment complexes, and luxury hotels. That strategy works particularly well for "America's richest landlord," 73-year-old Newport Beach Resident Donald Bren, the wealthiest man in American real estate. This self-made millionaire, with a net worth of $4.3 billion, made much of his money as chairman of The Irvine Company, a privately held real estate investment company known for creating balanced, sustainable, quality communities like the 93,000-acre Irvine Ranch in Orange County. Finished plots sell for more than $1 million an acre. The ranch also has 400 office buildings, 35 shopping centers, 80 apartment complexes and 2 luxury hotels. Bren is 6th wealthiest real estate billionaire and the 122nd richest man in the world. He is also one of real estate's great philanthropists.

**2. Do more than invest.** Making big money in real estate goes beyond buying property and waiting for it to appreciate in value. It's all about improvements or "adding value". John Sobrato of Sobrato Development Companies calls Atherton, home, but he made his fortune in Silicon Valley - for more than 40 years, Sobrato's SDC has developed real estate in Silicon Valley - specializing in facilities for high tech and R&D companies. Another self-made man, he began in 1953 with one of the first "tilt-up" buildings in Santa Clara County. Sobrato, who owns and manages the buildings it constructs and maintains single tenant occupancy, boasts a portfolio of $1.5 billion. His assets include land throughout Silicon Valley, San Jose, Fremont, Newark and Santa Clara and he has developed in excess of 7,000 rental units.

**3. Be able to see the property for what it could be.** Just because you buy a shopping complex doesn't mean that's the highest and best use of the property. Know the local zoning codes and be open to the possibilities...Los Angelino Ed Roski did just that. Roski is the founder of Majestic Realty, the largest commercial builder in Los Angeles, boasting an office, retail and industrial portfolio totaling more than 55 million square feet. The USC grad with a net worth of $1.1 billion saw the highest and best use of the formerly blighted area near the convention center and built the Staples Center with Philip Anschutz. Roski is also a minority owner of the Lakers and the Kings. Headquartered in City of Industry, Majestic Realty also has offices in Atlanta, Dallas, Denver, and Las Vegas - where they have a 400-acre business park and 3 million square feet of casinos.

**4. Be tenacious and relentless.** Billionaires don't let obstacles or pitfalls keep them from achieving their goals.

Newport Beach billionaire George Argyros is the grandson of Greek immigrants. Argyros began by running a Palm Springs grocery. He graduated to buying and selling corner lots at busy intersections for gas stations then turned to apartments in 1968. Today, as part of Arnel & Affiliates, Argyros manages apartments and commercial properties in southern California. He has a net worth of $1.2 billion.

**5. Have a thick skin.** People can be resentful and jealous of successful people. Don't let criticism of your work deter you from your goals. Consider Red Emmerson - the second wealthiest real estate titan in California. Emmerson is the largest private forestland holder in North America - assets include 1.52 million acres in Northern California, timberland stretching more than 350 miles from Mount Shasta to Yosemite National Park. For the last 20 years, while other logging companies retrenched or relocated, Emmerson, and his company - Sierra Pacific Industries - quietly grew into the second-largest private landowner in the United States. Needless to say, Sierra Pacific is a darling of environmental groups.

**6. Have superior information.** If you do more research than your competitors, you'll have an advantage in any transaction. Self-made billionaire Carl Berg was a loan processor before investing in Silicon Valley commercial real estate with John Sobrato in the 1960s. He struck out on own, forming Mission West Properties, a real estate investment trust (REIT) in Silicon Valley. Berg owns a controlling stake in the REIT, which focuses on single-tenant research and development and office properties in Silicon Valley. Mission West now owns and manages more than 100 properties, major tenants include Microsoft and

Apple Computer. Currently, the Atherton-based businessman boasts a portfolio of $1.2 billion.

**7. Don't accept the cards you're dealt.** Forbes notes that while one-third of the world's 46 billionaires who make their money in real estate inherited and then grew their fortunes, two-thirds are self-made. Stockton-based A.G. Spanos Companies are known for building, managing, and selling multi-family housing units; constructing master-planned communities, and developing land. Although California based, they have expanded to build more than 100,000 apartments in 18 states since 1960. A.G. Spanos Companies have also developed top-class office space in San Joaquin County. Alex Spanos, owner of the NFL's San Diego Chargers, operates the company with his sons Dean (president and CEO) and Michael Spanos (EVP). Spanos, whose net worth is $1.1 billion has pledged $200 million to San Diego for a new stadium for their football team.

**8. Live in California.** Of the 21 U.S. billionaires who made their fortune in real estate, more than one-third live in Atherton, Los Angeles, Newport Beach, Palo Alto, or Stockton.

**9. Get, and stay, married.** Of the 43 real estate billionaires whose marital status is known, according to Forbes, 37 are married, while only three are divorced and three are widowed.

**10. Go back to school.** Out of the 26 real estate billionaires whose educational attainments are known, 20 have a college degree or higher. Five made it on high school diplomas, and one is a high-school dropout. John Arrillaga is a big donor to alma mater Stanford University. Arrillaga + Richard Peery are two of 2 of Silicon Valley's biggest commercial landlords. In the 1960s, they converted farmland into pricey office space. Peery and Arrillaga are lifelong business partners who avoid debt, and the media. Each has net worth of $1 billion."

**11. Serve the Growing Population.** Based on the middle-series projections, the Nation's population is projected to increase to 392 million by 2050 -- more than a 50 percent increase from the 1990 population size. During the 1990's, the population grew by 27 million, a 10.8 percent increase. Only during the 1950's were more people added to the Nation's population than during the 1990's. Using the lowest assumptions, the population will grow slowly, peak at 293 million by 2030, then gradually decline. Conversely, the highest series projects the population to increase quite steadily over the next several decades, more than doubling its 1990 size by the middle of the next century.

**12. The Baby Boomer Time Bomb.** American statistics given by the Centers for Disease Control and Prevention and the Administration on Aging warn of the frightening economic implications brought about by a rapidly aging population. By 2030, the number of people older than 65 is expected to increase from 12.4% to almost 20%.

As money flows out of the stock market, the baby boomers will be looking for real estate investments, downsizing their homes, and getting rid of debt.

## The Art of Persuasion

The saying "No man is an island" is an undeniable truth. We need the support and cooperation of other people to help us in reaching our goals.

Successful developers know that one of the most important abilities to possess is the ability to persuade and influence others.

Here are some hot tips to do this effectively:

**Enter Their World.** Try to put yourself in the other's shoes and understand the situation from their point of view. Set aside your personal interests and concentrate on them. Ask yourself if you are them, what would you do? What would be your opinion? Then take the appropriate action that would be beneficial to them.

**Mirror Their Body Language**. People feel comfortable with those who are like them. Copy the person you are trying to create a connection with. Observe how they act, how they speak, and how they think. If they rub their forehead while they think, act like them. If they speak at a clear and slow pace, try to do the same thing. This is called mirroring. In due time, the people you're mirroring will subconsciously feel more comfortable with you. It's as if they see themselves in you. Proceed with caution, however. Do not let them be aware that you are copying them. They might interpret it as mockery and you'll just get into trouble.

**Be Cheerful and Nice.** Did your mother tell you to be nice to people? She was right. People like others who brighten up their day. Make a sincere compliment to raise their spirits. Little things like these go a long way to breaking the ice and setting the relationship off to a good start.

**Be Sincere and Trustworthy.** Make them feel that whenever they need help or just someone to look up to, you'll always be there to lend a hand. People tend to be more receptive to those they trust. If you have a boss or client you are trying to please, over deliver and exceed their expectations. Soon, they will notice your efforts and will be more than glad to grant your request.

**Provide Them With Compelling Evidence.** Explain to them how your ideas or suggestions could be the most effective techniques to implement. Show them undeniable proof that you have the best product by way of testimonials, before and after scenarios, and detailed comparisons against your competitors. Just make sure that all your claims are true and verifiable. Always maintain a good reputation.

**Show Them What's In It For Them.** This is the most important thing to remember when persuading anyone. People are self-centered. They always put their own well-being before others. No matter how close you are to becoming like them or how overwhelming your evidence is, if it does not satisfy the "What's In It For Me?" test, your persuasion efforts will not produce satisfactory results. If you can prove that your proposal will provide more advantageous benefits to them than to you, they are more likely to accept it.

**Genuinely Care For Them.** Focus more on their interests, desires, needs, and expectations, so you can satisfy their craving for attention, and establish mutual trust and respect. It also shows that you really care about them and that will make them more likely to trust you and want to work with you.

**Listen Carefully.** Skilled negotiators say that when you think you know the other side's view, you usually only know about one-third of it. Make it a point to know their position and the reasons behind it. Visualize the issue from their viewpoint to help you leas them toward your conclusion. Some experts say that pretending the person is a close relative or close friend helps you to understand their stance.

## Effective Negotiation

What is the meaning of "effective" in this context? Some people think that negotiating effectively means using whatever tricks, bluffs and ploys serve their purpose to obtain what they want from the other party, giving away nothing or as little as possible of their own goodies the other party may want.

This is not a realistic approach for serious professional business negotiators. Bluffs and tricks usually create a negative reaction. The "Machiavellian" approach is best left to unserious amateurs.

STUDENT: What do you mean by "Machiavellian"?

TEACHER: Machiavelli was an Italian statesman, historian, diplomat and political theorist. His famous treatise The Prince (written in 1513, published 1532), is a handbook for rulers. Though admired for its incisive brilliance, the book has long been widely condemned as cynical and amoral, and "Machiavellian" has come to mean deceitful, unscrupulous, and manipulative.

Anyway, the purpose of this course is not to teach you tricks and ploys to trap the people you negotiate with.

STUDENT: No? And why not?

TEACHER: Because as a businessperson you will usually negotiate with peers, not with gullible neophytes. These people will not be easily tricked. And many times your negotiations will be repetitive with the same party and you will not want to antagonize them by using bluffs and tricks which will jeopardize a mutually beneficial long-term relationship.

STUDENT: Then what is this course about?

TEACHER: This course is about realistic, effective techniques for getting the best possible results in serious, professional negotiations.

We will also teach you all known tricks, ploys and traps etc. But not to induce you to use them in serious negotiations. The aim is to prepare you for what the other party may throw at you, because "a ploy identified is a ploy neutralized". And we will also describe the basic types of tricky and difficult negotiators you may encounter, and help you to learn how to deal with them.

## Negotiating Ploys

**Just Under the Deadline.** This negotiator hands you a draft of the contract one hour before the deadline. He or she believes that, because you deadline is looming, you will be more likely to meet his demands. You can offset this by creating a deadline for contract review that is before you final deadline.

**Good cop/bad cop.** This is a team of negotiators, one of whom takes the hard core stand, while the other pretends to "make up" for his or her misbehavior. If this happens to you, consider calling them on it.

**The loyal employee.** This person plays one of two games, both of which can stall your negotiations. In the first scenario, he or she states that the offer should be acceptable to you because it is "standard". He or she might as well finish with, "you moron". In fact, nothing in real estate development is standard. The deal you are negotiating can be whatever the two parties agree to make it.

**I am not in charge.** The person claims they do not have the authority to make decisions or alter the terms of the contract. If this happens to you, simply stop and wait until someone who does have the authority can meet with you.

## One Final Word

If you are negotiating and you are not willing to walk away, you might as well stop negotiating and just hand over the terms the other party is asking for. Locking yourself in mentally before the negotiations put you on

the losing end.  You need to be willing to walk away –
graciously of course – if you want to get anywhere.

## *Key Points from this Chapter*

- Go commercial. Billionaires who make their fortunes in real estate don't do it in residential.
- Invest in growing areas. This was California in the 70's and 80's.
- Learn to be persuasive.
- Negotiate honestly and don't play games. You will have to work with these people again.
- Be willing to walk from a transaction, even if you are losing money.

# Chapter 9: Today You've Got to Have a Business Plan

How do you apply negotiating skills to your very first real estate venture to be successful and create profitable sales from the start?

Predevelopment is the period from your first glimpse of the development site to the beginning of construction. Ideally, this period would be only four or six months, which lowers both your cost and the risk involved. However, it is difficult to begin construction while the land deal is closing, especially for a developer who is working on a first project. So you should plan on a longer period for your project to take place. In the meantime, you must be sure you can carry the debt load that is required to make your dream a reality.

## Preparation

You should obtain a license to do business under your business' name. You have obtained insurance that offers adequate coverage for the task and retained an attorney to help sort out on all the many details that are involved.

An attorney finds the things that you might overlook. Look at it this way, you will get a bigger bill if you wait until you have a mess before you talk to an attorney. It is best to let a lawyer handle the things they know how to handle up front.

Getting good legal advice is necessary to set up the company properly. Remember, this is an ongoing process of making sure the company structure meets what the IRS wants to see as you hold properties and then matching this against what the local laws are for company structure. Get advice from both attorneys and your tax lawyers and weigh this against your top goals. But get legal advice on everything and don't take shortcuts.

One of the keys to a successful real estate development is preparation at every stage. As you become more experienced you will recognize questions and issues before they arise. For now, make the best preparation you can for every meeting and phone call that you make. For example, before you attend a meeting with clients, anticipate their questions and be ready with solutions. Before a meeting with the public, prepare answers and blueprints that spell out a response to their concerns. Before meetings with lenders, gather all the financial documentation and dates you think they will need. Anticipate the concerns of all parties involved as much as you can, and be ready to speak to their needs in their language.

Talking with other developers and studying their history will give you a fairly good idea of the questions that arise from all fronts, and the way that you can respond to them. Most developers agree that the best way to learn is to jump in and begin. There is no formula for success and there are no two projects that are alike. So it will be a learning process now and five years from now, even ten, and so on.

In any development process, there are different levels of risk to consider. For example, a low risk undertaking might involve you being an agent, managing a project for owners or investors. High risk might be investing all the money that goes in and out of the development and taking on all the personal liability. Most first developments fall somewhere in between.

Your first development will be the hardest on of your life. You will encounter more challenges, spend more time, and work harder than in any other development you set out to create, but know that once this one is behind you, there will never be another development as difficult, bewildering and time consuming. You will never again be a newcomer to the field. You will never have to create all the relationships necessary for the business or work so hard at getting clients, funds and approvals.

One word of advice: it is important to create exactly the type of business atmosphere you plan to have from the outset because the first development sets the tone for how you will do business in the future. You are establishing an image with people you will encounter again, including contractors, bankers and investors. So with that in mind it is important to:

- Do your research will and do not be tempted to latch on to the first development that you see
- Create a positive image
- Be as informed as possible before approaching the professionals you will partner with.
- Always behave in a courteous, friendly manner.

## Create a Business Plan

Every startup business has to create a business plan. The business plan consists of a narrative, several financial worksheets, and a summary. The narrative is the most important part.

Creating a compelling business plan takes several weeks. You will spend a great deal of that time researching, thinking, and writing. You will never be sorry that you created a thorough document for you business. But in this new economy, you have to have it for everyone involved.

The best way to create your business plan is to write out each section in paragraphs and edit it. A business plan is a valuable too because it forces you to research and think about your business in a systematic way. As you plan, you will think back over your ideas in a critical way, plus your research may turn up something that you did not know. So a well crafted business plan can actually save you time in the long run.

# The Key Problems With Most Business Plans (and how to eliminate them)

**Here are some of the common mistakes business owners make when completing their business plans:**

<u>Mistake 1:</u> Incomplete financials

This is perhaps the most important section of any business plan. Lenders want to know when they will have their loans repaid and assess the risk. You need to produce financial statements that accountants will endorse without question.

<u>Mistake 2:</u> Over ambitious projections

Everyone thinks their business will grow exponentially in the first 12 months but in reality this is rarely the case. Your business plan must show a realistic path to profitability that proves your actual revenues and profits are comparable with your written plan.

<u>Mistake 3:</u> Leaving something out

Every business plan follows a certain structure. Lenders and professional readers generally look for 3 or 4 aspects of your plan. You need to ensure you have these elements correctly written in the right area of your business plan.

<u>Mistake 4:</u> Incorrect format

Your readers do not expect a 100 page novel or a 1 page overview. Getting this fundamental area wrong will show your readers just how inexperienced you are.

<u>Mistake 5:</u> Poor understanding of marketing

Communicating your products to your prospects is a critical success factor for every business owner. You need to show you understand your target customers, what their needs are, why they will buy from you and how you will communicate with them.

<u>Mistake 6:</u> An inability to sell your plan

Having an accountant prepare your plan may save you a headache, but it is you who needs to explain to your lender or investors every question they have about your plan. You need to understand everything that is written in your plan.

## Financial Plan Outline

**1) Break even analysis**
One of the main financial objectives is to perform a break even analysis. This should be done before preparing the final financial plans for your operation. You should know the sales break-even point, that is, the level of sales necessary to meet the total business running costs. You can also use break-even analysis to determine the level of sales to achieve a desired profit target.

**2) Categorize costs as fixed or variable**
Fixed costs are constant. They do not change when sales levels change provided the business does not change its operating capacity.

Variable costs change proportionally to changes in business activity. When sale levels change, these costs also change (up or down). Examples of variable costs are stock purchases, raw material purchases, and direct costs (job material purchases).

### 3) Calculate the contribution margin

This is a key area of the financial objectives. The sales income of the business must be enough to cover its variable costs and its fixed costs as well as the required profit. The contribution margin is the excess of sales income over the variable costs of the business for the period (sales less direct costs). The contribution margin measures how much sales contribute towards meeting fixed costs and the desired net profit of the business.

This is the one of the key financial objectives, as without sufficient contribution margin you cannot meet your operating costs and you will be in negative net profit territory.

### 4) Calculate the break-even point

With a knowledge of the contribution margin (% to sales), you can find the business' break-even point, the level at which income equals expenses (direct costs and overheads or expenses), so that neither a profit nor a loss is made (in the net profit line of your profit and loss report).

### 5) Financial Forecasts sales

Sales forecasts should be the first forecasts made when planning profit and overall financial objectives. The sales forecast is of prime importance because it influences many of the cost forecasts for your business.

### 6) Forecast profit statements

Prepare a forecast profit statement showing the annual net profit target for the business for each year.

**7) Forecast capital expenditure requirements**

Prepare an annual capital expenditure forecast for each year. This shows details of your proposed capital expenditure for the period in the business plan.

**8) Forecast cash flow**

After you have prepared the forecast profit and capital expenditure statements, you can now prepare cash flow statements for each year of the business plan. Potential lenders will critically analyze your cash flow forecasts to determine your ability to meet loan repayments.

A cash flow statement shows the intended cash receipts and payments of the business over the period of the business plan, which then allows the cash flow to be calculated. A forecast cash flow statement shows the cash receipts (inflows) and payments (outflows) of the operation, which enables future cash positions to be predicted.

This is one of the key financial objectives of your business, and dictates any required level of funding over the coming trading period (budget year).

**9) Financial Ratios**

The calculation of financial ratios provides a useful summary of the acceptability of forecasts. They can be used to identify strengths and weaknesses in planned operating activities.

Ratios are compared with standard benchmarks such as industry averages for acceptability. Ratios should also be improving over time. The identification of any unacceptable ratios should cause you to review and adjust relevant sections of the operational plan to produce satisfactory forecasts and results.

**10) Financial records**

You will need to design a comprehensive record system

that records the financial transactions of the business. Financial records are necessary for the financial control of the operation. Records of financial transactions enable accurate reports to be prepared for monitoring the financial results of the operation. Financial results are compared with corresponding targets to identify any unsatisfactory performance so that follow up action can be taken.

## 11) Business insurance

Plan what types of insurance will be required for the business now and for the period of the plan, the types of insurance might include public liability (usually the minimum) and professional indemnity. Comprehensive insurance cover should be arranged and maintained for your business operation to minimize exposure to daily risks which can cause financial losses.

## 12) Financial controls

The final area of financial objectives is to establish the financial controls for your business. After you have designed your financial record keeping system, you should then decide what financial controls to adopt for your business operation.

Financial controls are the methods or techniques you will use to monitor and evaluate the financial results of your operation. Key financial results are 'profit', 'cash flow' and 'financial position'.

Understanding the financial objectives for your business operation is essential if your business is to be successful.

Many business fail because they do not take time out to first establish these, and then to monitor them. These are your "stakes in the ground" which ultimately support the structure of your business.

## Initial Ideas

This is the stage where you let the ideas flow, write them out, and sort them according to whether they can work.  As a good entrepreneur, you will find the opportunities that make money, hopefully ahead of the crowd.

Where do you get your ideas?  You can get them from a broker or from other developers.  You may talk to lenders or other people who are in the field, but you do not have to depend on other to show you where there is potential.  Drive around your area and spot trends as to what is going on in different areas.  Ask yourself where the growth is moving.  Is there an area that could be easily revitalized, or in which rehabilitation has already begun?  Is there an empty lot surrounded by rising commercial projects or one small farm being dwarfed by high condos?

Learning to anticipate the direction of growth will eventually make you wealthy.  At the idea stage, nothing is ridiculous and your market study will determine whether it is viable anyway.  Let your mind wander freely as you make a regular habit of assessing the area with business in mind.

Most cities do not tend to expand in an even pattern around their perimeter, instead, growth occurs along a corridor in a particular direction.  The person who can anticipate this direction and begin to develop property rights in this pathway is the person who will realize the greatest potential from his or her development.  Even if you hold onto a property for several years, if you are in the path of growth you cannot help but succeed.

Of course, if you choose to use a REALTOR to help you find ideas, a dedicated broker can be a wealth of information for you. A real estate broker knows what is for sale, what could be for sale soon and what simply cannot be bought. He has a clear idea of whether a property is a good deal and he is more than willing to share that information with you. If a broker feels you are a good buyer, one who will purchase the property and get to closing, he will work hard to find properties that meet your needs. Do not be afraid to let your broker know that you are new to the business and you want to start small. The more information you can give him, the more likely he is to find exactly the property that you want.

One caution, even when the broker prepares an attractive sales package, you should make it a habit to double check all the information he gives you. This is where a very hands–on approach pays off for a developer. What assumptions were made to put the package together? Are they valid? Are the figures correct? If he is showing you information about a tenant in a building, for example, go talk to the tenant. Visit with owners, city officials, and online sites that have provided the information he holds. Be sure that what the broker believes to be true actually is true. This habit will take you far and overcome some uncertainty in this business. In any case, make the broker do his work and don't ever just take an approximation, "Properties sell $100 per square foot range here...". Make him give you exact comparables and go look at the properties.

## Market Research

Market research is the starting point for any development. Before you can create a desirable product, you must fully understand your market and all its players and potential buyers/tenants. Building a project without first knowing the market can serve your own dreams and desires, but in the end it may not be very profitable.

My first commercial building was beautiful and took two years to build. The property was much too nice for the area though. I took people's opinions that it would lease for a price that was way above the competition in the area. Seven years later, I still haven't leased the entire building. Lesson learned. Do your homework.

The word "market" usually means groups of customers. They can be grouped and regrouped in many different ways – geographically, demographically, or by product type. It is useful to group them in these ways to study their needs and demands. For our purposes, the market consists of all you potential customers. They share a particular need or want, and they might engage in purchasing your goods or services if they perceive that those products supply their need.

Understanding the market means that you are aware of what your customers want and need. By understanding what they want, you can easily position yourself to offer production that will satisfy their demands. Therefore, as you may have guessed, your market study is an ongoing process. You will study your market as long as you remain in the business to establish what people want, and later to be aware of changes in those wants.

One example of the changing market is the way the U.S. household population has changed. Married couples with children comprised 80 percent of households in 1970; by 2003, only about 23% of households were made up of married families with children. At the same time, the number of single parent households rose from 11 percent in 1970 to 16 percent in 2003. These changes are significant if you are building residential dwellings, because the type of home that is required will be different.

By the way, as a developer, you cannot assume that because something is new and innovative, it will be successful. What is innovative may not be practical or it may not have appeal to the particular market you are striving to serve. If it does not succeed, cut your losses early and stop supplying it. Even experienced developers do not create their own demand through repeated supply.

A market study discovers whether the specific proposed project will enjoy future success. It involves developing and understanding of the local and national level of the market and its influencing factors. Trends can be used as forecasts of supply and demand. By understanding both levels of the market clearly, a developer or his marketing team researches and selects target markets using information on customers who have purchased or leased a product that is similar to yours.

When you are familiar with the national data, it is time to turn to the local market study. Let us begin with a study of the present trends. Examining local real estate ads, talking with brokers, and asking other developers will help you find out the types of space that are currently available. Look at their use and intended use, size, location, function, and style. What is similar to your idea?  What is different?  How do you think the differences affect the plan?

Next, look at the demand.  Demand is a fluid occurrence, meaning that it changes with trends and demographics.  What are current preferences telling you about your development?  Find the five most popular new developments in the area and study them in detail.  What is the typical unit size?  What are its features and benefits?

When you are comparing projects and doing market research, do not forget about the vacant lots that are on the market or sitting on the sidelines un-listed.  The possibility of competition is just as important as the current availability, maybe more so, since newer products (residential and commercial) may contain attractive design or other features that buyers and renters find appealing.

This is also the time to learn about rents and value.  What are the income levels of the typical tenant (buyer)?  Who are the buyers? In general, office occupancy rates are lower than the rates for apartments, generally a rate of about 90 percent for offices or 95 percent for apartments is considered acceptable.  What are the vacancy rates?  Working on a project that involves leases as an end result automatically means that vacancy rates are difficult to assess.  There are several reasons for this, but most likely there will be leases the developer may not be aware of, rentals that are not full to capacity, and the possibility of subleasing.  So it is best to focus on what percentage of space is being used by tenants, rather than try to calculate the vacancy rate.

How much turnover should you expect in a given time?  What are the operating expenses?  To provide any sort of building that fills a need, zero in on one type of development, for example, a high-rise apartment building, and learn everything you can about that project within your targeted area. Most of the above questions will be answered as the study progresses.

On the societal level, you will want to compare your market opportunity with all the forces that influence society and institutions, meaning you will study technology, demographics, political attitudes, legal changes, and economic trends. All of these studies should be ongoing if you are serious about a career in real estate development. By staying abreast of the trends, you already have a large part of your research out of the way. Reading Internet reports, ezines, newspapers, and industry publications will keep you up-to-date.

Another good way to gather information without a great investment of time is to locate industry forecasters and use their data. Forecasters pinpoint emerging trends and point them out, allowing you to use their projections to predict the robust side of the market and the trends in your area.

Do not underestimate the importance of networking with other professionals in the field, they have a great deal of knowledge.

On the Industry level, a market study includes current and potential suppliers, potential customers, and your competitors. It will also include a study of the politicians and the public, because these are the people who will regulate your market. Developers look for socioeconomic and behavioral distinctions that separate people into groups. This segmentation forms a distinct combination of people, lifestyles, purchasing power, and pace. For example, if you find that everyone who lives in a new development southwest of town is between the ages of 32 and 38 that is a pretty narrow segment. Obviously there is something attractive in the subdivision for that age group. What is it? Can you fill the same need for that age range? What is another target group that has similar needs? By studying these types of patterns, you will know the market.

Determine the ease with which a new project can be initiated in terms of local zoning and politics. The zoning and approvals process can take years, unfortunately.

Also note the size and any physical constraints such as drainage, soil conditions, and land formations like mountains or boulders, and bodies of water. Water should be a red flag on any piece of property and a signal that you can easily add a year on top of approvals. You will want to check the flood zones to see what the building envelope looks like as well and how this affects long-term financing.

Finally, you will measure your idea not solely against the market, but for its viability.

## Demographics

By comparing the actions of groups of people to historical patterns, we can see how trends are developing. The distribution of households with certain age, income, mobility, educational levels, and employment status is of particular use to developers who use the research to predict change.

Where do you find demographic information? You may have a local economic development office, city or regional planning center and state government offices. The bureau of Labor Statistics and the Economic

Research Service of the U.S. Department of Agriculture, and the National Planning Association publish estimates of demographics. If you cannot find demographic information, sometimes you can hire a consultant to perform a study for you, particularly if you are interested in a relatively small population, like a certain area of town.

Some demographic trends are easy to predict. For example, the high number of births in the United States between the 1940's and the 1960's spurred a demand for baby clothes and diapers, then a demand for education, and by the 1990's there was a dramatic rise in the number of retired persons. In fact, the elderly populations will increase by 80 percent over the next 25 years.

As a developer, you will be interested in studying the age and labor force of you area to follow trends and understand how lifestyles are changing. For example, baby boomers have created a more active lifestyle for retirement than earlier generations. Baby boomers have more disposable income, fewer children, and are more apt to own second homes. This information that definitely affects the size and type of home you would construct if you were a residential developer. However, match this with the current economic conditions, and you may have different ideas as a result.

Economic forces and wage rates create a pattern that changes over time. Studying trends gives you a forecast of demand for the market, and ultimately for you particular development.

## Regional Shifts

The residential future of cities and outlying areas determines the prevailing type of housing and business districts. Are secondary cities still growing? Does the main city show an increase in residents? How many residents are renters? Where do they tend to cluster?

The demographic shifts, urban sprawl, and a trend toward an environmental ethic have led to a trend called smart growth, which is an attempt to unify an area and avoid the segmentation of urban sprawl. It is the effort undertaken to restore communities and offer them numerous housing options by combining good environmental use with mixed properties – residential, commercial and retail. It helps to center the area on the town, giving the residents a renewed sense of place.

Smart growth preserves natural areas inside the cities as well as around the locality to give breathing room, wildlife, biological habitats, recreation, working farms, and environmental beauty. Open space preservation boosts the economy, supports the environment, and helps structure the new growth of existing communities. We will discuss more about smart growth in a later chapter of this book.

*This chart from the Social Security Administration shows the changes in age in our country for people turning 65 years of age.*

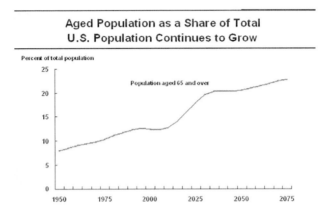

**Aged Population as a Share of Total U.S. Population Continues to Grow**

## Keep it Simple

As a beginning developer, you will probably want to choose a market that is close to home, so that you know the area and are familiar with local politics. The knowledge that you already have in the business will assist you in your success. A track record of successful small projects will take you far in the early stages of your career.

To create a successful first development, look for one that can be done in a relatively short period. Look for a simple deal in terms of acquisition and sales or leasing – one that is easily within your financial capabilities, even if that means bringing in a business partner. You will ensure success, which is vital at the front end of your career. Additionally, you will bring the deal to close more quickly and sleep better at night.

The governing body of the municipality often seems intimidating to the newcomer. Even if you are not a locally based business person (or you have not been up until now), with time and effort you can work your way through the political aspect of development. If you do not know how to play the game, you will learn. Land use is determined by local government, so you have no choice in the matter.

## STAGES OF REAL ESTATE DEVELOPMENT

| Planning Stage | |
| --- | --- |
| Feasibility Study | Design |

| Building | |
| --- | --- |
| Financing | Construction |

| Sales | |
| --- | --- |
| Marketing/Leasing | Operations |

## Viability

How does a developer know whether a particular piece of land is affordable by the project? What specific areas of information should a developer investigate after site control is achieved?

The business terms (price and timing of payment) for acquiring land for a development project is the most important decision that a developer makes because it is the only decision in the development process that the developer has complete discretion over making; if the price or timing of payment cannot be supported by the project, then the developer does not acquire. After the developer controls a piece of real estate the developer needs to focus expenditures on gathering information in areas of project risk and to continually evaluate whether the chances of success warrant further expenditures. If not, the developer needs to abandon the project and treat expenditures up to that point as a loss.

Factors that you will study are:

- Location
- Fit for the proposed use
- Accessibility
- Travel time and access to public transportation
- Public improvements
- Neighborhood factors, such as noise, crime, traffic

In determining the feasibility of a development, beginners try to go into too much detail early in the analysis. Remember, market analysis will take place both before and after site selection, so that you will have plenty of time to correct yourself as you move forward.

Developers always have to cope with the fluidity of the project. Developers are always worrying about having too little or too much data, having the market change after the initial market study or having inaccurate information. Part of your job on the first three or four developments you create will be learning to go with this constant movement, yet remain focused. By making a methodical effort from the beginning, you can stay focused on your goal. By staying current and networking, you will keep your eye on the market and its trends, and you will hear what other people have to say about your project. By returning repeatedly to the market study, you will be able to maintain control of your development process.

By projecting forward you will create a product that responds to future demand rather than the market demand at the time you began. Since the development process can take several years, changes will occur. Where will the economy be in three years? In five? Who is developing the property around your proposed site? What are they building? How will that tie into your plans? Are they a competitor ore will the other development fit awkwardly against yours? These are all questions that help you consider the future market demand. It is prudent to learn all that you can and to keep yourself informed of the changes around you as they occur.

If you are developing land, at this stage you will want to contact firms that build your type of product. They will be a great resource for your feasibility study. You should also contact brokers and lenders who stay current on local market trends and will offer tremendous insight into the feasibility of your project.

## *Key Points from this Chapter*

- Money, location, and time are the three areas of focus that make a successful real estate project. Make sure you have a solid plan for all three areas.
- Write your Executive Summary last. This is the most important part.
- In the new economy, you will be judged by the quality of data you base your assumptions on. Investors, bankers, and clients will be looking at this. Make sure you stand behind it.
- Understand how you are going to reach your target market. Just because you build something doesn't mean they will buy it. You have to have a marketing channel to them. Show this cost and plan in detail.
- Do your research. Don't ever show something in your proposal that you haven't researched.

# Chapter 10: Transaction Based Real Estate Business

As discussed in earlier chapter, I couldn't finance any properties at a reasonable cap rate and loan to value in Utah toward the end of the boom. Instead of grinding it out and refusing to work until the market conditions change in my favor, I decided to modify the way I did business. Instead of having an equity position in real estate, my business partner and I focused on matching bank owned properties with investors that were in the $2 Million to $5 Million price range. Our role was to manage the project for a consulting fee. Usually the properties were foreclosed townhome projects or vacant residential subdivisions that had been fully improved. These sorts of transactions provided the chance to develop an expertise in the local market, serve banks and investors, and afforded us the opportunity to earn a very lucrative salary.

As with any professional endeavor, the most important factor in generating new business is to remain honest and ethical during all your business transactions. Everything else tends to take care of itself. Protecting your reputation and being known for your professionalism, business acumen, and competence will eventually pay huge dividends.

I know a very astute investor from Denver who was buying apartment complexes a decade ago throughout that city. Eventually, he launched a real estate brokerage firm and located it in one of his mixed-use buildings. After a few years, he had about 20 sales agents working for him and founded a property management team. He basically had a lock on his farm area because the majority of local sales and rentals went through his firm. Here's how:

- He would cherry-pick the best deals to buy before they made it to the general market.
- He would always show his apartments (before showing units from other owners) to prospective tenants who called his office inquiring about vacancies.
- He used market intelligence that he gathered from his active team of brokers to get ahead of the curve on almost everything that would affect his business.

In sum, this shrewd entrepreneur had a self-made competitive advantage over everyone else.

One of my investors moved to Phoenix to escape Utah winters. He used to own apartment buildings here in Utah. The business he began, is a hard-money lending firm specializing in funding investors that are rehabilitating unfinished bank foreclosures. The problem he solves is the complete lack of financing available for uncompleted homes. No bank will lend on these, because they don't know what the value is. He does. He's making several points and 12% interest for a six month term.

Another good friend from the Midwest owns more than 3,000 apartment units and nearly half a million square feet of retail and office space. According to him, the market had been slow for new transactions during the past few years, so he developed a new side business that has compensated him extremely well during the past 12 months. "Chad, I've bought and sold 45 mortgages in the past 11 months for a net profit of $1.4 million."

One past business partner that was developing office condos for doctors, switched gears and is now leasing units to doctors and selling the leased space to investors with an incredibly cheap cap rate and everyone is winning. He informed me that his brokerage business now represents more than 50 percent of his company's annual revenue. He's still an equity player on deals, but the buildings he buys require 3 to 10 years to develop and sell. The brokerage business, however, provides steady and consistent cash flow year after year.

The primary advantage of owning an active brokerage business or working as a transactional broker is that it can serve as a major cash cow that pays your monthly expenses. Brokerage businesses tend to have modest overhead but can produce a significant amount of cash flow. Unlike equity plays, the brokerage business doesn't require your own investment capital when you're working on a deal. You can earn commissions upward of 6 percent (or more) of the transaction price. In fact, you can sometimes forfeit your commission and trade it for an equity position in the deal. If you want to maintain a good pulse on the market and be involved in deal flow, I highly recommend being in the real estate brokerage business.

## Case Study

Paco Diaz is the senior vice president of retail properties at CB Richard Ellis (CBRE). He is known as "The Big Box King" of Miami. He leases the largest retail spaces in town and has been doing it successfully since 1983.

During the boom era, he was extremely active, and his deals were closing rapidly. Land was moving quickly, and retailers were opening stores at a fairly good rate. Projects that were dormant for years suddenly came alive again. In fact, 2005 was the very best year in his illustrious career. "I couldn't do anything wrong," Paco said. That year, he sold a very large parcel of land to a national shopping center developer and sold several other large projects. He was ranked the number 1 retail broker for CBRE nationwide. Paco admits that hard work, local knowledge of the market, a laser-sharp customer focus, and a bit of "good luck" made him successful.

However, good times always come to an end. In mid-2008, it all changed. Banks stopped lending; retailers stopped expanding; developers stopped buying land; vacancy rates in shopping centers lingered. Paco's listings –which just a year before received multiple offers – now received very few offers. "It seems like it occurred almost overnight," Paco said.

He continues to represent both retailers and landlords – working both sides of the equation. He is still oriented toward the bigger deals rather than smaller ones. He works harder and smarter that before, and deals take longer to get done. Paco says he just doesn't have the luxury to waste time, so he's highly selective about how he dedicates his time during his workweek.

He predicts that the market will start improving by mid 2012, when banks begin lending again and employers start hiring. According to Paco, the future will look like this:

- Lots of cash on the sidelines waiting to buy.
- Banks will have to bite the bullet and sell properties
- Owners will sell at a discount.
- Higher prices will follow when the economy improves.
- Every property is different – so location is critical.
- "C" and "B" rated properties must offer big concessions and lower rents to attract tenants.
- Grade A properties will be in much better shape to ride out the downturn.
- In fact, rents will be in much better shape to ride out the downturn.
- The low end retailers will remain very healthy. Subway, Dollar Stores, T.J. Maxx, and so on are all making money.
- There are no new locations to move into because there's no new development.

His last words of sage advice: "Take good care of your clients throughout the downturn, and you'll do well when the economy recovers."

## *Key Points from this Chapter*

- The market will start improving by mid 2011, when banks begin lending again and employers start hiring.
- Banks will have to bite the bullet and sell properties
- The primary advantage of owning an active brokerage business or working as a transactional broker is that it can serve as a major cash cow that pays your monthly expenses.
- There are opportunities to help people with real estate, especially in this market, using your background knowledge and charging a transaction fee.

# Chapter 11: Commercial Real Estate

During the past four years, I've been waiting patiently for the collapse of the commercial real estate sector (in particular, retail and multifamily) so that I could start buying again. A quick study of previous real estate cycles shows that a downturn in the commercial sector historically follows the unraveling of the residential market. In fact, most real estate experts agree that commercial real estate is the next shoe to drop in this ever-changing world of ours.

In early 2010, a Congressional oversight panel for the Troubled Asset Relief Program (TARP) stated (on record) its opinion about the future of the banking system as it relates to commercial real estate:

Over the next few years, a wave of commercial real estate loan failures could threaten America's already-weakened financial system. Commercial loan losses could jeopardize the stability of many banks, and as the damage spreads beyond individual banks, it will contribute to prolonged weakness throughout the economy.

With commercial property values declining by nearly 40 percent since 2007 (resulting from higher vacancy rates, lower rents, and increasing concessions), it is estimated that about 50 percent of all commercial real estate loans will be under water by the end of 2010. Making matter even worse, $1.4 trillion in commercial real estate loans will mature in the next four years, and many of the borrowers won't be able to refinance into fixed long-term loans.

## The Retail Sector

The adage in retail real estate is that, "Retail follows rooftops". Shopping center developers tend to follow residential builders. As single-family homes, condominiums, and townhouses are constructed and people move into their new dwellings, shopping center developers follow soon thereafter. But rest assured that, when rooftops dwindle, retail is not far behind. Retail has always been largely dependent on residential real estate as its engine and primary source of growth. I prefer infill retail projects near established residential, office, and industrial projects – in proximity to the places where people live and work.

As unemployment increases, consumer confidence dwindles, and families begin losing their homes to foreclosure, the demand for retail space declines. Think about it this way, if you fear losing your job because everyone around you is being laid off, aren't you going to reduce the number of times you eat out at expensive restaurants, get you haircut at the salon, and buy new clothes at your favorite shop?  During lean times, everyone cuts back on unnecessary expenses.  Individuals will dine at home more often and avoid eating out.  They might launder their own clothes versus dry-cleaning them, and, perhaps, they'll extend the time between visits to the hair salon.  They will delay or cancel the purchase of a new plasma TV or washer/dryer.  As consumers reduce their discretionary spending, retailers feel the direct impact to their bottom lines.  Retail sales decline because consumers won't spend as much as they had in the past.  Eventually, retailers aren't able to keep up with their expenses, and they close shop.  The same holds true for the office sector.  Do you think the local accountant, physician, attorney, or other professional will expand his or her office or lease additional space while such economic uncertainty looms overhead?  Do you think large corporations will expand their operations to other cities if their sales are sliding and they are forecasting lower revenues?

The depressed economy has created a rise in commercial vacancies that has affected property owners' ability to maximize net operating income (NOI).  The owners of retail and office assets find themselves at the mercy of the existing tenants because of the fallout.  Many tenants who managed to survive during the downturn are requesting rent abatements (a reduction in rent for a specified period) to weather the storm.  It's a vicious cycle in which overleveraged investors find themselves under a great deal of duress – especially the commercial property owners who made acquisitions at the peak of the market.

Lower property values result from higher vacancy rates, lower rents, and the subsequent drop in property's NOI. Investors who purchased a commercial property in 2002 to 2008 likely wished they hadn't. Their properties are probably worth less than what they paid for them. Moreover, they're unable to refinance their mortgages without making a significant capital contribution to pay down the existing debt and achieve an acceptable loan to value ratio.

A commercial real estate crisis will wreak havoc from 2010 through 2014, as commercial mortgages come due for refinancing on projects that are under water. Risk-adverse lenders aren't willing to refinance existing debt unless the ratios are in line with the lending standards established by the new economy. These conditions are taking a heavy toll on owners of apartment, retail, office, and industrial buildings. The new economy – with its constricted credit markets – has made it impossible for many property owners to refinance their loans.

Here's an example. Let's assume that in 2006 you acquired a large shopping center for #100 million. You bought the property with 20 percent down (or $20 million), so your principal mortgage balance is $80 million.

The property performed well until 2008. That year, however, brought new challenges that you hadn't anticipated. For example, you began to notice red flags that included new leases being signed at a 20 percent discount compared to leases signed for similar space just 12 months ago. Vacancy rates increased as you lost tenants to the souring economy. Existing tenants requested a reduction in their rents, and you were obliged to give it to them to keep them in place. New prospective tenants demanded significantly more tenant improvement allowances (TIAs) than what you had offered to any other tenants since acquiring the property.

By late 2008, you're barely breaking even with all the financial obligations associated with the property. The loan on the property will mature in 2011, and you owe more on the property than it's currently worth. Let's assume that the property is now worth $60 million based on the most recent appraisal, but you still owe $80 million. Your equity (that $20 million you deposited on closing day) has disappeared suddenly, and you don't qualify for refinancing because your lender has adopted tighter lending standards and will accept only a 75 percent LTV on the currently appraised value. You quickly do the math and realize that the bank will offer you only a $45 million loan. To refinance, you'll need to make up the difference – a whopping $35 million in cash.

You're wondering whether you should make the next mortgage payment once you realize that the possibility for your situation to improve is rather bleak. You become less motivated to continue making payments on a property that's only worth $60 million. (Don't forget, you owe $80 million) You'll soon be bleeding money, and you certainly don't have an extra $35 million sitting in your bank account for the refinancing. When the loan matures (assuming you make it that far), you'll be faced with two options.

- Come up with the $35 million to refinance.

- Give the property's keys back to the lender and fight out a deficiency in court.

This scenario is by no means far-fetched; it will be a nightmare repeated for many property owners throughout the country. Thousands of commercial property owners will find themselves in financial dire straits in the next four years. In fact, total commercial real estate losses are estimated to exceed $300 billion.

The chief economist from CB, Richard Ellis, recently made the following comment to the *New York Times*: "Anyone who purchased (commercial) property in the past six years has their equity pretty well washed out." (Charles V. Bagli, "Buying Landmarks? Easy. Keeping them? Maybe Not", January 16, 2010). As I'm writing this chapter, I find myself in the midst of negotiating a deal for the acquisition of a 51 lot subdivision from an extremely distressed developer. We've been waiting on the sidelines for many months now, and it's finally time to be building on this property. The developer at one time had several subdivisions under construction and was doing extremely well. He had over $2 million of his own money in the project. We will be buying the property on a short sale from the bank at less than what the property development costs were. The problem is that he bought the property back in 2006, then took two years entitling and putting in curb and gutter. He got though one phase with successful sales, but then the market hit the skids in 2008 – hard. The bank revalued the property and needed $1 million to keep the loan in conformance. He let all his properties go back to several banks.

## What to Expect

Since building values have declined so much and lending standards have become incredibly more stringent, disposition of properties for at least the balance of the outstanding loan is, in many cases, not a viable option. Furthermore, refinancing is no longer an option either. Developers can't sell their properties for what it cost them to build, so many are exploring the possibility of negotiating a short sale with their lenders to get out from under the exorbitant debt that they can't possibly repay. Others are attempting to convince their lenders to extend their loans with the hope that the market eventually will rebound in their favor.

The problem is expected to mount as more loans mature and as the economy continues to languish. After all, no one expected nearly 50 percent declines in property values and the worst recession since 1929. I would argue that the short-term implications for the commercial real estate industry are alarming and that many property owners (particularly those who paid a premium during the past few years and financed their acquisitions with short-term debt) ultimately will lose their properties to foreclosure.

Most industry experts estimate that commercial loan delinquencies will peak in 2012. In the meantime, lenders may deal with the problem by reworking the troubled loans or extending their maturity dates. The primary advantage for banks to extend loans is that they don't have to "mark to market" assets on their balance sheets. Mark to market refers to the assignment of the current market price to assets on the books while recognizing the loss. Most lenders prefer to avoid foreclosure because they aren't in the business of property ownership nor do they want to alarm the FDIC, so they might try to extend the maturity date of their troubled loans to give the borrower more time to figure out a solution. The industry refers to this activity as "extend and pretend" because the lenders extend the loan and pretend they won't have to take a loss on it.

Lenders will consider the term of a loan to avoid writing down the value of the asset – that could be as high as 50 percent. Eventually, however, the FDIC will force lenders to clean up their books and take losses by selling their nonperforming loans or owned inventory of real estate to investors at steep discounts. Once the federal regulators and/or lenders decide that loan extensions are no longer working, the floodgates should open and investment opportunities will likely abound for the patient capital that's been sitting on the sidelines waiting for the commercial market to hit bottom. But until both lenders and owners accept the new valuations on their properties and sell at existing market prices, a large-scale recovery is unlikely to occur.

## *Key Points from this Chapter*

- Developers can't sell their properties for what it cost them to build, so many are exploring the possibility of negotiating a short sale with their lenders to get out from under the exorbitant debt that they can't possibly repay.
- A commercial real estate crisis will wreak havoc from 2010 through 2014
- The depressed economy has created a rise in commercial vacancies and will result in lower values.
- It is estimated that about 50 percent of all commercial real estate loans will be under water by the end of 2010.
- $1.4 trillion in commercial real estate loans will mature in the next four years, and many of the borrowers won't be able to refinance into fixed long-term loans.

# Chapter 12:  Retail Real Estate

Retail real estate includes shopping centers, strip malls, outlet centers, and so on.  The usual suspects to lease retail space include national tenants such as AT&T, GameStop, Starbucks, McDonald's, Wendy's, Great Clips, Auto Zone, 7-Eleven, The Vitamin Shoppe, Chipotle, and large, big-box, national retail tenants (often referred to as anchor tenants) such as BJ's, Home Depot, Target, Best By, OfficeMax, Staples, Michaels, Toys "R" Us, and the granddaddy of them all – Wal-Mart.

Retail tenants are categorized into the following three groups: national chains, such as Subway, that has more than 31,000 locations worldwide; regional concepts, such as Upper Crust Pizzeria with 20 locations in the Boston area; or "mom-and-pop" businesses such as Ted's Dry Cleaning company that may service a local community with only one store.

The 10 largest franchise systems in the United States are:
1. Subway (22,227 locations nationally)
2. McDonalds's (12,127)
3. Mani-King (9,713)
4. Curves (7,091)
5. Burger King (6,343)
6. Jazzercise (6,280)
7. Ameriprise Financial (5,853)
8. Jackson Hewitt (5,853)
9. Dunkin' Donuts (5,213)
10. Pizza Hut (5,084)

As reported by FRAN data, the fastest growing new franchises include:
1. Healthsource
2. Instant Tax Service
3. SuperSlow Zone
4. Auction It Today
5. Premier Rental-Purchase
6. Math Monkey
7. Guard-A-Kid
8. World Properties International
9. Cellairis
10. DNA Services of America

# Retail Demand

The need for retail property in a given area is dependent on the local household demand for goods and services. The aggregate demand for retail space nationally is dependent on specific consumption patterns (i.e. what people need) and overall consumer demand.

Consumers place a premium on value and are extremely price-sensitive during tough economic times. In fact, discount retailers that offer more affordable alternatives such at TJX Companies (T.J. Maxx), Costco, BJ's Wholesale Club, Ross Stores, Kohl's, Dollar Stores, and Target have been some of the nation's best retail performers during this recession. In fact, these companies are experiencing some of their most profitable quarters in decades.

# The Past, Present, and Future of Retail

The following is a conversation I recently had with a retail property owner. The owner said,

> My father acquired this building in 1964, and I've owned and managed it since 1978. This is the worst retail market I've experienced since we've owned the property. Our current rents have been reduced to 1986 levels, and we need to offer significant incentives to prospective tenants just to keep our occupancy at a decent level. Making matters worse, prospective tenants who want to lease vacant space from us can't obtain financing because of the constricted credit markets. It's just a horrible retail market right now.

As previously mentioned, investors who acquired retail real estate during the past six to seven years likely paid a premium –as they did with most other asset classes during that period. Investors bought on inflated pro-formas that projected rising rents, declining vacancies, understated concessions and tenant improvement allowances (financial incentives given to new tenants to offset their up-front expenses). Retail investors not only overpaid during the past seven years, but they used significant leverage (75 to 95 percent loan-to-value) and short-term debt to make those acquisitions. Convincing banks to lend the vast majority of the capital required for commercial property purchases was not problematic in the old economy.

During the boom, most retail investors pursued the same exit strategy. They'd buy and existing center or build one from the ground up. They'd make much-needed capital improvements on the existing center or complete construction of the new development. Afterward, they'd lease all the available space, stabilize the asset, and maximize the property's net operating income (NOI). Finally, they would sell the property for a handsome profit and immediately begin the search for the next project. Assuming they could execute the plan within the time allotted, their loans would not mature, and millions would be made after the sale. It was a relatively straightforward and lucrative strategy, if the market cooperated and the investor was reasonably competent.

Unfortunately, the market did not cooperate after 2007. Although the subprime debacle contributed to the collapse of residential real estate, the subsequent financial crisis was responsible for causing aftershocks in the commercial market – including retail real estate. When the current recession began to negatively impact retailers, shopping center owners began to feel the pinch. After all, when individuals lose their job, home, and hope for the future, they naturally stop spending. AS consumer sentiment waned, so did retailers' income. A clothing store retailer shared the following with me: "I've been in business for 25 years and have always done well. During our very best years from 2004 to 2007, we generated about $100,000 a month in revenue. Our revenue is down 70 percent in 2010. We've never seen anything like this. I'm not sure how much longer we can stay in business.

Eventually, thousands of retailers were forced to close their doors, and vacancy rates skyrocketed at shopping centers throughout the country. When the economy began its downward tailspin, businesses in general became leery of future expansion. It suddenly became increasingly more difficult to fill vacant retail space. National retail vacancy levels reached an 18 year high of 10.6 percent in the fourth quarter of 2009, according to real estate research firm Reis.

Even highly profitable retailers that wanted to expand could no longer secure the financing required to open new stores. One of the problems was attributed to the faltering of the nation's largest source of credit: CIT Group Inc. provided financing to about 1 million small and mid-sized businesses but filed for bankruptcy in late 2009. The credit market for most retailers evaporated almost overnight and additional credit, therefore, no longer existed for store expansion. Moreover, no one has been able to fill the void left behind by CIT's departure from the marketplace.

Existing tenants have been requesting rent abatements from their landlords to survive the recession. Furthermore, prospective tenants have been demanding much lower base rents and significantly larger tenant improvement allowances (TIAs). Retail vacancy rates have been climbing while rents have been falling. All in all, the situation is bad for retail property owners, and it's only going to get worse before it improves.

One of my friends is the principle of a firm that owns more than 1.5 million square feet of retail space. He stated that his strategy for 2011 was essentially tenant retention. He wanted to maintain a 90 percent occupancy rate in his centers. The mandate he was passing down to his leasing agents was not to lose any more tenants! The primary emphasis wasn't on new leasing or increasing rents but, rather, on the retention of the existing tenant base.

Nevertheless, because many property owners can't sell their centers for more than the debt owed on them and refinancing isn't an option, the entire sector will continue to experience sever contraction. Until the employment rate improves and consumer and business spending increase, I don't anticipate a recovery in the retail sector. The recovery is unlikely to occur until 2013, or, even later. That said, it's a great time to be buying if the numbers are right and you have patient money.

## Consolidation

Expect the weak to be gobbled up by the strong. Investors with strong balance sheets and deep pockets will acquire companies that are unable to refinance their debt and are in poor financial condition (because of the dramatic deterioration of the market conditions).

Simon Property Group Inc., the largest mall owner in the country, made a $10 billion offer for General Growth Properties Inc. (GGP) in 2010. This acquisition did not materialize but would have resulted in the coupling of the nation's two largest shopping mall owners. General Growth declared bankruptcy in April 2009 after several failed attempts to refinance its debt. Once again, too much leverage and too many overpriced acquisitions during the past few years are to blame for the company's downfall. Indianapolis-based Simon Property Group Inc., owns 382 properties in North America, Europe, and Asia and could make the acquisition using almost all cash. This is the epitome of Darwin's theory of "survival of the fittest".

The consolidation would have created a near monopoly in the high-end shopping center sector. Most retailers were not in favor of this merger because they feared the overwhelming leverage a Simon/GGP union could have wielded in the marketplace. For instance, a retailer might be forced to lease at multiple centers just to gain access to a single location it truly desires. Also, rents might be artificially inflated in shopping centers if one company owned the majority of the nation's retail space at these traditional shopping centers.

## Challenges of Owning Retail Real Estate

The U.S. retail sector is not for the faint of heart: Many small retailers find it impossible to compete with Wal-Mart and Target.

Small retail stores are also facing increased competition from Internet retailers. The Internet reduces expenses for online retailers when compared to brick-and-mortar retailers. Many online retailers are not subject to increased operating expenses in the form of commercial property insurance, taxes common Area Maintenance (CAM) charges, annual rental bumps, employee salaries, and sales tax.

Moreover, it takes an average of 4 to 9 months to lease commercial retail space.

Novice commercial real estate investors don't realize the costs associated with securing a lease with a good-credit tenant. Assistance with the build-out cost (i.e. tenant improvement allowance) can run to tens of thousands of dollars alone.

## Pop-Up Stores

I recently spoke with the director of leasing for a Simon Mall property, and he offered me two options: Temporary leasing and permanent leasing. Property owners have discovered that they can fill unused space with removable kiosks and vacant space with temporary merchants. It has truly become a win-win situation for all parties involved.

One of the most recent trends for retailers is the pop-up or temporary store. Pop-ups have been instrumental in filling mall space during this economic slump. Pop-ups allow for short-term leases that could last 3 to 24 months. It offers retailers the luxury of being able to test concepts, locations, and product lines to determine whether success will follow. Retailers avoid signing a long-term lease that could prove financially disastrous if a particular model doesn't work.

Sometimes, it just doesn't make good business sense to sell year round. After realizing that almost all of its business took place during the holidays, Hickory Farms moved almost exclusively to temporary stores and kiosks. Toys "R" Us and J.C. Penney use pop-up stores extensively throughout the United States.

## Case Study

*Matt Miller.* "The coming commercial crash." <u>The Deal Magazine</u>

*January 9, 2009*

In early November, General Electric Co.'s General Electric Capital Corp. moved to foreclose on a downtown Phoenix office building in a hearing scheduled for February. The 18-story office building is just another one of those nondescript rectangles that seem to punctuate the skylines of city centers across the United States. The owner: a San Diego company with the innocuous sounding initials of BCL Inc. The foreclosure makes that Phoenix office building special, in a gloomy sort of way, and a harbinger. Throughout the U.S., massive numbers of foreclosures have swept through residential real estate. By contrast, commercial real estate foreclosures remain relatively few and far between, even in cities the economic downturn has hit hardest. Bankruptcies are even rarer.

"Lenders don't want to default. Borrowers don't want a default. So lenders have extended to the extent they can," says independent real estate investor Terri Gumula. "Everybody's holding out."

The fate of the building on 111 West Monroe Street then is a "precursor," says Christopher Toci, executive director for Cushman & Wakefield of Arizona Inc., of what he and others expect is a massive problem to come.

"It has the potential for being a God-awful mess," adds David Jones, a longtime real estate attorney with K&L Gates LLP of Charlotte, N.C.

Right now we are witnessing what in many respects may prove to be the proverbial calm before the storm. Commercial real estate owners will soon face gale-force winds on two fronts. The rapidly deteriorating real estate market has only recently hit commercial properties. More critically, loans issued in the boom years are only now coming due, with little or no prospect of refinancing. "The velocity [of distress] is going to increase tremendously," says Ed Casas, managing director for Navigant Capital Advisors LLC, which advises hedge funds and private equity on distressed real estate. "It's just begun."

Just how bad the destruction will get is difficult to say. No one predicts the kind of unprecedented devastation residential real estate has experienced, where subprime mortgages alone, which reached $600 billion in 2006 and formed the underpinnings of several trillion dollars in mortgage-backed securities, collateralized debt obligations and credit default swaps, created vast wastelands. But the commercial mortgage failure numbers could be staggering as well.

"What worries people the most is that even healthy assets can't get refinanced," says Dan Fasulo, managing director of New York research firm Real Capital Analytics. "There's so much dislocation in the debt market. It no longer has the capacity to refinance all the loans that are coming due."

Real Capital Analytics considers about $21 billion worth of commercial real estate in distress, while almost $81 billion worth of additional property faces potential troubles in 2009. In all, roughly 5,000 individual properties are on Real Capital Analytics' watch list. Fasulo believes his current forecast errs on the conservative side.

Others believe the numbers could get much higher and that distressed commercial property in potential default may actually exceed $400 billion. Everyone expects the crisis will worsen in 2010 and remain nasty through 2011. "There will be a significant increase in default rates of commercial mortgages," says Stephen Tomlinson, senior partner in the real estate practice at Kirkland & Ellis LLP. But "you may not see a spike begin until the fourth quarter."

Christopher Grey is managing director and co-founder of Third Wave Partners LLC, which both invests in distressed real estate and advises investors. He predicts it will take three years (from 2011) before the market begins to recover. "There's a tremendous amount of adjustment to be made, but very little adjustment has taken place," he says.

There are ominous signs. The CMBX Indexes, which track 25 tranches of commercial mortgage-backed securities, now show "an unbelievably wide spread," says Grey, with an implied default rate of 20%.

Unsecured REIT bond spreads "are at all-time highs," Fitch Ratings Inc. reported in an outlook last month, which tagged office, industrial and retail REITs with negative outlooks. The stock market has already hammered commercial REITs, many of whose market caps have declined by more than 90% in a year. One dramatic example of a REIT teetering on the edge is General Growth Properties Inc., America's second-largest mall operator. General Growth narrowly avoided bankruptcy last year, when it was able to extend $900 million in debt repayments until February. General Growth still faces huge uncertainties with billions of dollars of short-term debt maturing soon.

Understanding why commercial foreclosures have lagged so significantly behind residences helps explain a great deal about what transpired during real estate's boom years. What's likely to happen in 2009 and 2010 offers a sobering look at assets that were considered robust and fairly safe until the fourth quarter of 2008. Now they are poised to become yet another part of the economic devastation.

Working through all this distress will be extremely difficult and time-consuming. Wrapped within those numbers is an often complex jumble of securitizations, debt tiers, priorities and liquidation preferences. In the best of times, these make decisions and workouts difficult. Now it's even more daunting.

Most of these properties are in bankruptcy-remote vehicles, which make it easy for lenders to take back assets without bankruptcy filings. What's more, current laws discourage commercial real estate-related bankruptcy filings. So it's more likely that borrowers would be inclined to just give up the keys and walk away.

However, most lenders don't want the property back, since there are few potential buyers. Money for refinancing remains almost nonexistent. With securitized assets, lenders are often at odds with each other on what course of action to take, depending on what part of the debt structure they fall. "It's a recipe for short-term paralysis," Casas says.

Commercial real estate encompasses everything from the toniest retail shopping complexes to modest strip malls, from low-rise office buildings to luxury hotels and skyscrapers. All face huge problems.

What's more, the economic distress will be wide-ranging, not just in the boom towns of California, Florida or Nevada, but in cities that stretch north to south and coast to coast, lawyers and commercial real estate advisers around the country say. "It's the same phenomenon all over," says Andrew Schwartz, a Boston-based partner at law firm Foley Hoag LLP. "The trouble is nationwide."

Schwartz cites his city as a prime example. In the past few years, real estate consortia paid huge sums for trophy properties. At the same time, star-crossed developers unveiled ambitious new developments. Now several major projects are on hold, including the $2.5 billion Fan Pier development and the $700 million redevelopment of the storied Filene's department store site. Developers can't get construction loans. At the same time, landlords of existing properties face rising vacancies and an inability to service loans.

Or take Phoenix, which was "one of the poster children for subprime mortgages," Toci says. That led to overbuilding in retail shopping centers and suburban office complexes. "A lot of [commercial] projects that were planned have either been reduced or are in trouble. One project in Tempe, a boutique hotel, just stopped," says Jeffrey Pitcher, a Phoenix-based real estate partner at Ballard Spahr Andrews & Ingersoll LLP. "We're at the stage where developers delay as long as possible the construction."

But Toci believes it's the economic downturn that is really doing his city in. "We've lost 58,000 jobs through November, and now Phoenix faces an oversupply of offices," he says. Tenants are going bankrupt, vacating properties or not renewing leases. "Operationally, there are serious weaknesses. Commercial real estate is just starting to tank."

Nearby Las Vegas is the site of one of the worst examples of residential speculative frenzy. Long after the housing bubble burst and residences were foreclosed on a massive scale, the city thought its economy safe, given its dependence on gaming and tourism. So ever-more-opulent casinos, upscale shopping centers and multibillion-dollar multiuse development projects continued to launch. But the economy has wreaked havoc on Las Vegas. That in turn has put enormous pressure on the city's livelihood.

"It all started feeding on itself," says David Barksdale, a Las Vegas-based partner at Ballard Spahr and the co-head of the firm's distressed real estate initiative. "Now it's spreading into the commercial side."

The city's most dramatic foreclosure to date came in September, when Deutsche Bank AG took over the $3.9 billion Cosmopolitan Resort and Casino project after developer Ian Bruce Eichner defaulted on $900 million in construction loans and the bank couldn't find willing buyers. But many more problems loom. Several new office complexes sprang up in the southwest part of the metropolitan area.

They broke ground two to three years ago, when "things looked great," says Barksdale. Now they're completed, but deserted. "Those buildings are empty," he says. "Those are see-through buildings."

Atlanta, on the other hand, thought itself relatively immune to commercial real estate pain. Not anymore. "I foresee a lot of commercial deals going sour," says Nicholas Sears, an Atlanta-based partner at Morris, Manning & Martin LLP. "Folks want to sell. They can't sell. Purchasers can't get new financing or assume existing debt, which can't be reduced."

Even a city like Milwaukee, which hardly went crazy during the property boom, is feeling the effects. "Banks have closed down their lending. Ninety percent of commercial lenders are just not lending right now," says Nancy Haggerty, a Milwaukee-based partner at Michael Best & Friedrich LLP. "Even some long-term lenders like life insurance we're just not seeing any more."

As the crisis unfolds, there will be inevitable comparisons to the savings & loan crisis of the late 1980s and 1990s. Easy money created a speculative boom and massive supply in commercial property, followed by a banking failure, a wholesale takeover of distressed properties by the federal government and a yearlong sorting out. Professionals, however, caution against a quick analogy.

"A lot of people are trying to draw parallels to the early '90s, but I think it's certainly a different animal," says Martin Caverly, a Los Angeles-based principal at private equity real estate fund O'Connor Capital Partners. Unlike two decades back, there isn't a huge oversupply of commercial property, except for retail, he explains. But the ownership structure of property is far more complicated and opaque, with crippling debt structures and a lack of affordable financing, which make workouts and disposition difficult.

"More and more my belief is that it will be a larger and deeper correction," Caverly says. "The deleveraging process will go on for quite a long time."

What's certain is that in terms of debt to value, many commercial properties of various shapes and sizes are well underwater. "From a 90% loan-to-value, it's now a 130% loan-to-value," Tomlinson says.

Transactions are pretty much stalled right now. Grey estimates commercial deals in 2008 declined 90% more than in 2007. Even distressed players are in no hurry to buy. At a real estate conference late last year, a panel of private equity principals divided their world into two camps: Those with properties admit they're overbought and want to sell. Those with cash are sitting on their hands.

"It's very much a wait-and-see," says Pitcher. Potential buyers "want to see where everything settles out. They're looking, but they don't know where the floor is."

The shift has been dramatic. In early February 2007, Blackstone Group LP paid a staggering $39 billion for Equity Office Properties Trust. Most of the 100 million square feet of commercial real estate was financed by debt. During the next six months, Blackstone recouped $28 billion by selling off a little more than half of the properties. That included $7 billion New York property mogul Harry Macklowe forked out for some prime Manhattan real estate. Macklowe financed his purchase primarily through bridge loans from Deutsche Bank. At the time, Blackstone's maneuver was hailed as a brilliant model of leveraged deal making: Buy a property portfolio with short-term debt and quickly reduce debt levels by offloading a portion of the properties.

The music stopped in June 2007, when the credit crunch hit. Macklowe, for one, flamed out in spectacular fashion. He was stuck with loans he couldn't service and hugely overpriced real estate he couldn't hold. Deutsche Bank ended up taking back seven properties, selling five for huge losses. The sale of the other two fell through, and they are back on the market.

The Blackstone-EOP deal, it turns out, represented the last great hurrah. How Blackstone will dispose of its remaining properties is as yet unanswered. "They can't sell that stuff," says a rival PE investor. "There's not enough debt on the planet to float those trades."

In fact, the kind of flips Blackstone pulled off had been popular at least since 2005, when commercial real estate really began to heat up. The returns were equally dramatic as the Blackstone-EOP shuffle, although not necessarily on the same mega-scale. Biltmore Holdings LLC, for example, bought the 111 West Monroe Street building in Phoenix along with a vacant downtown redevelopment site in April 2005 for $20 million. After investing a further $6 million in upgrades on the office building, Biltmore Holdings sold the two properties for $52 million in February 2007. BCL paid $40 million for the building alone.

Why commercial real estate, which mirrored residential real estate, boomed is easy enough to understand. Financing was plentiful. Securitization was commonplace.

In some ways, the more expensive the asset, the easier it was to finance the purchase.

Why the collapse of the commercial real estate market didn't occur sooner is equally obvious: cash flow. Tenants filled buildings and paid rent. Because the terms of most loans were anything but onerous, as long as borrowers made interest payments, they were safe. "Rents haven't backed up far enough. Vacancies haven't ballooned high enough" to reach crisis point, says Richard Hollowell, a managing director with Alvarez & Marsal Real Estate Advisory Services. That won't happen for another three to six months, Hollowell believes.

"Until the fourth quarter of 2008, you didn't see a significant deterioration of property fundamentals. Even deals done at the top of the market were covering debt service with cash flow or reserves," says Tomlinson. "Defaults won't materialize until reserves are depleted, and they can't [cover debt service]."

Even through the summer of 2008, with credit markets frozen, there wasn't the kind of wholesale panic that was sweeping through residential real estate, and a false sense of hope prevailed. The Macklowe debacle wasn't repeated, and more optimistic observers viewed it as an outlier. "Overall, businesses were treading water. Underlying fundamentals were holding up," says Gumula. Commercial real estate owners "could make their debt service, so defaults were rare."

All that changed after the mid-September financial meltdown. "Up until Lehman, we were pleasantly surprised by tenant activity," she says. "Yeah, deals took longer to get signed, but up until September, plenty of leases were getting done."

Since then, it's been a dramatically different story. The economic downturn began take its toll on commercial occupancy rates. Typically made for three, five or seven years, commercial real estate loans are coming due, with few financial institutions willing to offer refinancing even at onerous terms. The combination can be deadly.

In boom days, borrowers could regularly obtain 90% financing. Those days are long gone. According to a Cushman & Wakefield Sonnenblick-Goldman LLC survey last month, the few financing deals quoted or completed were typically 60% loan-to-value.

Retail complexes were the first to exhibit signs of distress. That makes sense, since many shopping centers got whacked by both the residential real estate meltdown and the more general economic malaise. With the residential real estate boom came exurban sprawl. "One of the first amenities is a neighborhood retail center," Jones explains.

After the subprime crisis, however, residential developments were stillborn. The population that retail developers had expected never materialized.

Local retailers find it increasingly difficult to pay the rent, and they close stores. The retail developer defaults on an existing loan. He can't refinance, because there's no retail stream. A lender is forced to take that property back but doesn't want to because there are no buyers.

"It's a daisy chain," Jones says. "In some ways it's related to residential real estate, in some ways it's related to the general slowdown of the economy. The two feed off each other. It's a race to the bottom."

Shopping centers may have been the first to go. But it's the huge trophy acquisitions that are poised to cause the largest headaches. "A tremendous number of assets were bought in '06, '07, using short-term money. These were megadeals," says Casas. Now they're coming undone.

When Casas is asked to name those transactions that must be restructured, his partner, Neil Luria, pipes up with "any building sold within the last two years." Luria, a Navigant managing director based in Cleveland, is sitting in the lobby lounge of the Waldorf-Astoria Hotel in Manhattan. He gestures outside. "Just walk down the street," he says. "L.A., Chicago, New York, all the major markets have a number of high-profile trophy properties that will go through major turmoil. They are dropping precipitously in value, 40% to 50%."

Securitization enormously complicates these large transactions. Residential mortgage-backed securities may dwarf the amount of commercial mortgage-backed securities issued, but $40 billion worth of CMBSs is due this year, $55 billion in 2010 and $73 billion in 2011.

Like pools of residential mortgages, big commercial mortgages were sliced and diced into various bits and pieces. A single building may have a dozen different tranches of debt. Senior debt alone may have been parceled out into a dozen different pieces. Those pieces could have been combined with other commercial mortgages.

The complex financing structure makes the most fundamental decisions difficult. The senior-most debt holders may want to foreclose, since they're still in the money, even with a highly distressed sale. But junior debt holders would be wiped out in such a sale, so they'd be much more likely to choose some kind of restructuring and resist foreclosure.

Who makes the decisions complicates this even further. In normal times, a servicer is responsible for collecting interest payments from the borrower and distributing that money to lenders, with amounts dependent on returns within the various risk levels. So, for example, a senior lender may get 5% a year, while the junior-most doubles that.

If a borrower defaults, however, the role of the servicer is replaced by a so-called special servicer. That entity is appointed by the junior-most debt holders still in the money and is often an affiliate of the lender. The special servicer's loyalties and desired course of action may be very different from the senior lender.

You can imagine what a workout meeting looks like. "To get 50 partners together to work at a deal for pennies on the dollar, forget about it," Fasulo says.

Expect plenty of litigation to follow, say some lawyers (naturally). "More junior classes are not going to go quietly," says Schwartz. "Hedge funds playing with other people's money are not going to go quietly." Schwartz foresees a rash of valuation-oriented litigation. Servicers, especially, "are treading in very treacherous waters," he says.

Bankruptcies don't appear to be a particularly good alternative, either, especially for owners. After the S&L fiasco, when developers routinely put their bad properties into bankruptcy while keeping their good projects, loan contracts now carry what are termed "bad-boy" clauses. These state that owners can be held personally liable for their bankrupt properties.

Pretty much all the securitized buildings are housed in special-purpose entities. Because they are single-asset LLCs, they get only 90 days from the time they file to fashion a reorganization plan with a good chance of success, or creditors can petition the court to lift any stays. That kind of timetable isn't at all realistic in these times, when just finding debtor-in-possession financing is a major undertaking.

One of the very few property-related bankruptcies so far focused on a Chicago property called Hotel 71. The complicated case was anything but satisfactory. Distressed private equity shop Oaktree Capital Management LLC actually tried to foreclose on the equity of the holding company. The developer put the company in bankruptcy to prevent foreclosure. At that point, secured lenders of the actual property commenced a second foreclosure, this one of the hotel itself. The lenders eventually carried out an auction. Bids were well below value. "We ultimately decided to take the property back," says Brad Erens, a Chicago-based partner with Jones Day, which represented the special servicer.

Erens, for one, believes commercial property-related bankruptcies will inevitably follow. "At some point, borrowers will file. We just haven't seen it yet."

But Tomlinson counters that the bankruptcy-remote structures coupled with the bad-boy-type springing guarantees will "significantly dampen foreclosures that turn into bankruptcies." He adds that bankruptcy judges will probably have to rule on the legitimacy of bankruptcy-remote vehicles. "I think they ultimately will be upheld," he says, but cautions: "There's no playbook. A lot of things will be done for the first time. Literally."

What could really bring the crisis to a head is a crackdown by regulators on financial institutions demanding they clean up bad loans. If regulators demand lending institutions revalue the assets that secure the loans and institutions demand that borrowers fork over a hefty percentage to pay down the loan, financial institutions will have to foreclose.

Even now, banks are taking a chance by holding on, says Barksdale. If they modify the loan for 12 or 18 months, "they might have an asset worth significantly less," he says. But if they foreclose, "no one is buying."
Or offers they do extract may be going for a quarter of the value banks have on the books, he says. To date, the impetus has been to do nothing, if at all possible. "Things will continue to be pushed out until there's pressure from the outside accountants and regulators," Hollowell says.

Only when owners can't pay their debt will lenders be forced into action. That was the case with 111 West Monroe Street in Phoenix. Principals at BCL didn't return phone calls seeking comment. But those familiar with the building's fate say BCL defaulted after an equity partner collapsed.

That partner: a bankrupt firm called Lehman Brothers.

## Gone Are the Days

Gone are the days when developers would just build a shopping center and wait for tenants to fill the space. No one is speculating on new retail space anymore. The only existing construction and development projects being built today are for specific users. A couple of years ago, retail developers needed approximately 10 percent down or zero percent down in some circumstances. Now, they need 30 percent or more, and their being required to come up with that amount of equity has become a major roadblock for most developers.

In a severely down market, value-add deals don't work as they once did. You shouldn't buy a center, make massive capital improvements, and then raise the rents on your struggling tenants. During a recession, tenants can't pay higher rents. Instead, stabilize your property and concentrate on the operating expenses as well as the retention of your existing tenants. Do what you need to do to cut costs until the economy improves.

## Opportunity

Banks most certainly will consider making more commercial loan modifications because they don't have too many options other than becoming commercial property owners themselves. Inasmuch as banks are in the business of lending, most prefer to avoid direct ownership of real estate assets. Even if the monthly payments made to the lender are reduced, most banks will realize it's better to receive some form of payment – with the hope of eventually receiving a full repayment of the balance owed – rather than receiving no additional payments, foreclosing on the borrower, and being forced to liquidate at a significant loss (not to mention the legal fees involved). Many commercial borrowers might be able to eventually get back on track and pay off their loan. It therefore might benefit banks in the long run if they would be more amenable to loan modifications, especially if the economy is still lagging and the alternative options are not as favorable. Collaborating with borrowers to find a solution may be the bank's most prudent option.

If commercial lenders opt to extend loans that have matured and are in default, don't expect a bevy of distressed-buying opportunities in the retail sector. If, on the other hand, lenders decide to cut their losses, mark to market nonperforming loans, and clean up their balance sheets by liquidating, it would likely represent a tremendous opportunity for well-capitalized investors to identify distressed properties and acquire them at a significant discount to their fair market value. Buyers who can purchase and hold assets will most certainly profit when the market rebounds.

If you acquire a retail property that is not stabilized (i.e. less than 80 percent leased), you must be financially capable of weathering the storm until capital markets thaw out, consumer spending improves, and retailers begin to expand again. If you don't buy low enough and/or you use too much debt (assuming you can even source financing) for your retail acquisitions, you might regret making the acquisition too soon.

Either way, if you can acquired well-designed, well located retail centers at steep discounts using a reasonable amount of debt, you will undoubtedly do extremely well in the next market cycle. Long-term products for the asset class are quite favorable, but the horizon for brighter days is still 3 to 4 years away. Yu must buy low enough so that the numbers make sense for you today and during the next few years because vacancy rates and rents will continue to slide. Be conservative with your analysis of prospective acquisition targets, and assume that the market will not rebound for a few more years.

## *Key Points from this Chapter*

- Many property owners can't sell their centers for more than the debt owed on them and refinancing isn't an option because banks aren't lending.
- The entire sector will continue to experience sever contraction.
- Tough times for retailers has meant lower rents for property owners. This has meant lower values on their properties and posed a barrier in refinancing loans that are due.
- The foreclosure scenario we are seeing in residential housing will be scene in retail commercial real estate lasting through 2014.

# Chapter 13:  Office Real Estate

In December 2006, an acquaintance of mine purchased a 10,000 –square foot office building on 70,000 square feet of land for $13.3 million.  The property included 105 parking spaces.  Three weeks after the closing, he received an unsolicited offer for the property of $15 million.  Unfortunately, he couldn't convince his business partner to accept the offer – and a quick and headache-free $1.7 million profit.  His partner was confident that a much bigger payday would be earned if they waited.

Within a few months, the owners negotiated a letter of intent to sell the property to Marriott.  Marriott's plan was to convert the existing building into an extended-stay hotel for business travelers. The profit on the Marriott deal was a healthy $4 million, a much larger payday, as predicted by his business partner. Unfortunately, the market conditions began to deteriorate in 2007, and Marriott decided not to proceed with the transaction. The owners then were forced to consider alternative plans for the site. They concluded that a mixed-use property (residential and retail) would provide the best use for the site. A residential condo project of 200 units was proposed with several thousand square feet of ground floor retail. But that plan never materialized because of their inability to secure construction financing in a tight credit market. In the meantime, the vacant building sat idle collecting dust but still incurring ongoing expenses that included maintenance, taxes, and insurance. To make matters worse, the building was vandalized, and the air conditioning systems were stolen. The vandals severely damaged the roof while extracting the air-conditioning units, and the rain subsequently poured into the building causing even more damage to the interior of the property.

The mortgage was extended in December 2007, December 2008, and then again in 2009. Each time their lender agreed to an extension, they required the borrowers to pay down the loan with a substantial equity payment and provide additional collateral. The most current appraisal, however, had the property valued at only $3 million.

At this point, the owners had failed to make mortgage payments for 90 days and are officially in default. Because the borrowers don't have any additional capital to apply to the mortgage and they can't refinance the property because it's only worth $3 million (the still owed $7.1 million), the lender refused to extend the loan again. The borrowers are convinced that their only option now is to find a buyer and convince their lender to accept a short sale at a steep discount. A short sale or not purchase, however, presents its own set of unique problems. They will probably still be responsible for the deficiency (the difference between what is owed and what is paid to the bank) and could be pursued by the lender or buyer of the not. Also, in the even the lender forgives the amount not paid back, the IRS will classify the deficiency as a taxable income. Last but not least, the borrower's credit will be damaged by a short sale to the tune of 200 to 300 points.

## Bringing the Deal to the Lender

Banks and special servicers are inundated with problem loans. Note sales remain the lender's best way to dispose of nonperforming loans. If a lender has lost its patience by continually extending a loan, it should be more receptive to a short sale. In fact, the lender's eagerness to sell a note at a discount might be more acceptable by a bank's board if the bank already extended the loan numerous times and has lost hope that a less costly exit strategy is forthcoming.

Most "bottom fishers" tend to think that the opportunity to find a distressed property will avail itself to them directly through the lender. However, what many inexperienced investors neglect to consider is that, when the bank makes the determination to sell a nonperforming note at a discount, the manager of special assets will contact its top five to ten customers and, unfortunately, you're not likely on that list.

Alternatively, you should be speaking directly with the distressed property owner so you can bring the property, your offer, and the owner directly to the lender in one easy-to-analyze offering. Working in unison with all the parties that have a vested interest in the asset will improve your chances of doing a deal. Moreover, you'll bypass the lender's top ten buyers because special assets will feel obligated to work with you. After all, you're bringing them the deal even before their loan officer sees it. I'm speaking from experience. This really works.

## Opportunities for Doctors and Lawyers

For many entrepreneurs and small business owners, the question of whether to buy property or to lease office space can be a confusing issue. If you ask a professional real estate broker, he or she will probably tell you that it depends on the particular situation. It's usually a good idea to purchase a property when you know you'll remain in a location for 10 years or more, especially if you think you can get the property at a below-market price.

However, if you are short of capital to acquire a commercial real estate office space, well then the decision is made for you. In any case, leasing could perhaps be the most intelligent move. Statistics confirm that most new business owners start out by leasing office space. Furthermore many business consultants advise leasing commercial real estate office space particularly until you get on your feet and your business starts operating in the black.

A qualified broker will be able to execute a lease vs. purchase cost analysis that will help inform your decision. However, always double check with your tax consultant to make certain that your decision is favorable from a tax perspective.

Aside from general office space, specialized industries such as manufacturing or life sciences that have heavy and unique infrastructure requirements are generally better off buying their space. If you have to spend a lot of money to outfit a building to meet your needs, you want to own those improvements. Warehouse and distribution facilities, on the other hand, are interchangeable and can usually be leased cost-effectively.

Here are some advantages to purchasing your commercial real estate property:

- **Invested Equity.** If you think you can get your property at a below-market price and will be there more than 10 years, purchasing your property may be worth your while.
- **Debt Service & Tax Benefits**. This can make owning more advantageous than leasing.

Advantages to leasing your commercial real estate property:

- **Flexibility.** One obvious advantage to leasing property is the flexibility it provides. When the lease is up, you can easily relocate to another office that better suits the needs of your business and your budget.

- **No down payment**. When you purchase a building, you typically pay 20 to 25 percent of the price as a down payment and then mortgage the balance. When you lease office space, you need only pay one or two months of the lease value before moving in, which can be a real blessing for cash-strapped small business owners.

So, if you're a professional and you are going to be in your space for a while, right now you can buy space for less than it would cost to build the space. The financing is a dream through the Small Business Administration offering 90% financing and in most cases you can get all your Tenant Improvements (TIs) included. After ten years, you are still paying the same amount in monthly payments, but you also have equity from paying your mortgage down and the increase in the property value.

Here is a graph that shows this scenario where you buy an office condo in your area and rent back to yourself:

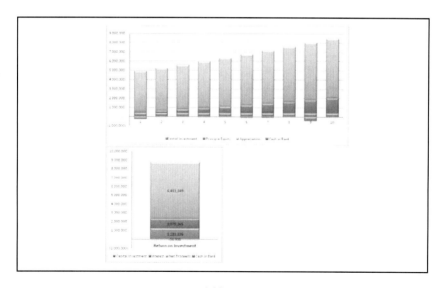

This same play can be done buying an entire building that is mostly rented out and renting one of the spaces back to you.

## Case Study

San Antonio's office market has been relatively flat in recent years, but one segment is seeing some sparks. Office condos, the latest trend in commercial real estate, are selling well.

"It was the smartest thing I ever did," says Dr. Lane Walsh of his decision to buy office space for his dental practice rather than continue to rent.

Walsh bought his property on Sonterra Boulevard more than a year ago when rental costs and lease negotiations became unacceptable.

"I started out with an office where the rent was $1,600 for about 2,100 usable square feet," he explains. "After seven or eight years, my rent was up to $3,550." Walsh adds that he'd been trying to negotiate a new lease for more than a year but kept being put off.

"The leasing agent was playing the waiting game – waiting until I was near the end of my lease and out of time to look for another place before it ran out," he says.

Walsh is one of a growing number of professionals, primarily health care providers, who have decided to become their own landlord. One of the factors driving that decision is the cost of retrofitting office space for medical usage. Physicians, dentists, and other health care-related businesses have specific and extensive electrical and plumbing needs. Doctors are often willing to put up with rent increases and additional pass-through costs because they're reluctant to leave an office once they've put several thousand dollars into making it fit their needs.

"Now any improvements I make belong to me and not the landlord," Walsh says.

"When you put $40,000 into customizing a space you're renting, the landlord will usually amortize it over the length of the lease," explains Dr. Craig Kuebker. "Then they'll want you to sign at least a five-year deal to make sure they get their money back."

Kuebker, a family practice physician, shares his recently purchased office on Huebner Road with Drs. Frank and Cheryl Mueller, a husband-and-wife team. Monthly expenses were a factor in their decision to buy as well.

"This was one of the few overhead expenses we could do anything about," he explains.

Sharing ownership of their building wasn't a risk for Kuebker and his partners.

"We share a waiting room in our rented office for about 15 years so we knew each other pretty well. We get along fine so there was no problem making the commitment to own our office space," he adds.

Jim Ploetz, marketing director for Huffman Developments, says the main reason professionals are buying their offices is because they can. "Previously, doctors who wanted to own their own office space would either have to buy, or at least buy into, an entire building. That leads to another entire array of investments. Now, in a campus setting, they can buy just the space they want to occupy. If they want to buy 3,000 square feet, now they can. At the end of the day, they want to have a hard asset that they can say, 'this is not only my office, it's an investment.'"

Not all owners are single tenants. Brian Harris, vice president of transaction services and a partner at REOC Partners Ltd., says many owners find tenants to lease any spare space they have in order to cover their mortgage costs.

"Doctors and dentists see this as an income source too," he explains. "Say they're in their 30s or 40s. They can easily go to a bank and finance this. They tend to be good risks and real estate tends to appreciate so the bank may lend them a higher percentage."

Investors buying multi-tenant buildings are usually able to finance about 70 percent of the purchase. As a single-tenant owner or majority tenant, Harris says buyers can finance up to 95 percent of the building's cost through the Small Business Administration (SBA) and as much as 80 percent through a commercial bank.

"So a doctor buys a building and he occupies it for 10 or 15 years and decides to retire. He can sell his practice to a young doctor and retain the real estate and lease it to his new tenant or he can sell them the practice and the building and walk away."

## Value Added

Having a hard asset like a building to include in the deal may make it easier for a retiring doctor to sell his practice. Kuebker says times have changed in the 15 years since he bought his practice after retiring from the Air Force.

"Practices aren't really worth anything when you retire anymore, especially among primary care physicians. Most people belong to PPOs (Preferred Provider Organizations) now so they don't get to choose their doctor. And patients have gotten used to switching doctors so I can't tell a young doctor that I have 3,000 patients to turn over because they might not stay. The facilities are something tangible that comes along with the practice."

So far Huffman is building two developments: The Villages on Sonterra with three buildings, which are occupied by physicians, an attorney, a mortgage company and insurance agent; and The Villages on Huebner, with two buildings up and another set to open in July. That location is being acquired by dentists and physicians.

Other developers are entering the office condo market as well. Local developer Efraim Abramoff is building condominium offices at the Huebner Town Center, located at the corner of Huebner Road and Churchill Estates Boulevard. Last year, Alcar Construction began working on a 10-acre development at Huebner Road and Stone Oak Parkway targeting health-care businesses that want to own their own offices. Earlier this year, TC Austin Properties and Alfra Development of Laredo teamed up on a project that includes office condominiums.

## Not for Everyone

But buying office space isn't a no-brainer for everyone. Steve Nathanson of the Nathanson and Nathanson Accounting Firm says every situation is different.

"It's a matter of what you can afford. If you pay $500 a month rent now, can you really afford to pay a $2,000 mortgage in order to own your own building? You have to paint a worst case scenario. 'If I have no business and no tenants, can I afford the mortgage?'"

He also advises potential buyers not to assume there will be tax advantages to owning their office. Commercial property is depreciated over a period of 39 years, according to Nathanson and a portion of the cost of the space is allocated to which appreciates.

Business people should also be aware of the lifespan of their business. Short-term businesses, likely to last less than five years, will not be able to fully depreciate the cost of a building and are advised to rent space.

"I own my own building," Nathanson explains. "And I'm glad I do, but it's not right for everyone. I basically stole my place at an auction and I also have a couple of tenants, which helps. But this is a third-generation business. We've been in business since 1953 and I expect to be here for a long time to come."

Another factor Nathanson tells potential buyers to consider is the cost in dollars and time of property management. Huffman Developments uses professional maintenance services at his properties paid for through association dues.

"It's like being in a homeowners' association," says Walsh. "You're responsible for your office but the grounds and the parking lot and any common areas like sidewalks, they belong to the association. You pay your dues and the association manages all that."

Ploetz says that most office complexes, such as the Villages on Sonterra, which has just begun construction on its second phase, hire association management companies although it's possible for building owners to manage the property themselves.

"We offer a turnkey operation," Ploetz explains. "We sell our office space in two phases. We sell the office as a shell and then we sell the interior. It's like a custom home. I can tell you what the outside is going to look like, but it's up to you to decide where you want the interior walls and the plumbing."

Ploetz says business people have the option of building their own offices. "I've had people tell me they can do it themselves and why should they pay me. I tell them, good luck. Call me for the grand opening. I know what it takes to do this. I know what it takes to buy land, make sure it's zoned properly, get it platted. Then they have to come up with an architect and builder, develop plans, etc. You can see the hours invested. If I'd spent all that time and money to become a doctor, that's not where I'd want to spend my time."

"Regrets?" asks Walsh after being in his office for more than a year. "Only that I didn't do it sooner."

"We're still grinding out the punch list," laughs Kuebker, "like any new owner. But we're happy with the space. I wish we had done this long ago but it was just so much easier to rent 10 or 15 years ago. Today, even after you negotiate a lease you're not sure what you're going to be paying because of the pass-through costs. This is the right thing for us now."

## Case Study

A company named Keystone Property Group with expertise in the office market, had acquired a 300,000 square foot office complex in 2007 and was in the midst of executing its value-add plan to the property. Keystone buys office buildings that are well-located but poorly leased and require significant capital improvements to attract higher-paying tenants. In other words, Keystone buys Class B or C properties in A areas. It buys the properties at a discount; makes the requisite upgrades, and leases at higher rents once the renovation has been completed. When existing tenants' leases expired, Keystone offers to extend their lease at higher rents once the renovation has been completed. The operational expenses for the property are reduced as much as possible while the rents are increased. Once the property has been stabilized and its net operating income maximized, it's time to sell. This strategy yields enormous profits and has been successfully repeated over and over again by Keystone.

After the tech-wreck and terrorist attacks in 2001, the office market was severely crippled. By 2003, the economy began to improve, and the demand for office space followed. Rich Gottlieb, a senior vice president at Keystone and a seasoned veteran with the company, survived several of the market cycles in the past. As Rich explained, "The office business is all about employees. The demand for office space is dependent on the economy. If the economy sours, so does the office market. It's a cyclical business with many ups and downs."

During the boom, however, the value-add cycle (the time it took from acquisition of value-add deal to its disposition) was reduced from 5 years to 24 months. Because of the compression in the deal cycle, Keystone earned phenomenal returns from 2003 through 2007. By early 2008, however, the conditions started to change for the worse, and 2009 was an extremely challenging period. Gottlieb noted, "The market has been going down, and pro formas are now thrown out the window. The objective is to keep properties filled at current market rents."

Apparently, 2009 was a decent leasing year for Keystone, but the leases signed were at much lower rates.

When asked about the future, Gottlieb remained optimistic that the conditions for his business would improve within the next 12 to 24 months. "Companies need to make decisions for future growth. Companies have cut back very deeply, so I don't anticipate it getting much worse. Hopefully, we will turn the corner by 2011."

He did admit that numerous challenges confronted his firm in the new economy. "The rules have changed," he proclaimed. The capital markets and debt side of the business are not what they used to be. Very few lenders have an appetite for speculative developments (i.e. poorly leased properties in need of capital improvements). Banks just aren't lending for acquisitions on un-stabilized properties. Without the ability to finance these types of properties, Keystone and other investors in the office sector can't achieve the returns they want; therefore, their value-add business model no longer works.

Keystone has had to reinvent itself in the new economy. It now is searching for less risky deals that don't required as much capital but would benefit immensely from Keystone's leasing expertise. Keystone hopes to buy office assets at reduced prices from motivated sellers; aggressively pursue their leasing plan; and ride future cap rate compression. Although Keystone wants to buy distressed assets from banks, they're not seeing any deals at the moment. Lenders are pushing loans out further and aren't foreclosing on office buildings. Gottlieb admitted that, "Banks are, in fact, better off extending for now. They still remember how much money investors made during the RTC days, so they want to get their money back this time around. We are not anticipating many distressed deal opportunities but continue to aggressively look."

Keystone's existing inventory remains problematic as well. The strategy during these tough economic times is to keep the properties leased and well maintained. Profits are eroding, but it's better to accept lower lease rates while minimizing vacancies than to suffer through this period with fewer tenants resulting from an attempt to maintain high lease rates. They have asked all their banks to extend their loans. So far, all of them have agreed. "They're not going to take down good sponsors," Gottlieb noted. That said, the new loan terms come with higher rates and required more collateral and additional equity payments to ensure their downside risk.

## *Key Points from this Chapter*

- Very few lenders have an appetite for speculative developments (i.e. poorly leased properties in need of capital improvements).
- The objective is to keep properties filled at current market rents.
- On short-sales, working in unison with all the parties that have a vested interest in the asset will improve your chances of doing a deal.
- Banks and special servicers are inundated with problem loans.
- Professional like doctors and lawyers can buy their own space in today's market far below what it would ever cost to build the space. This could be one of the best opportunities in the marketplace.

# Chapter 14:  Residential Real Estate

History will forever link the current housing crisis to an abundance of easy-to-obtain debt and subprime loans.  Because subprime borrowers used exotic loans (i.e. adjustable rate loans with 1 to 2 year teaser rates, negative amortization loans, and so on) to finance mostly condominiums and single-family houses, the value of residential real estate has fallen precipitously since the crisis began in 2007 – a year that coincides with the first wave of those loans resetting to higher rates.  Although the residential market was the first to falter, it will likely be the first to rebound when the economy recovers.

The run-up in residential prices was caused largely by the government's manipulation of the markets and its deregulation of the financial industry.  After the dot-com bust and the terrorist attacks on the World Trade Center in 2001, the Federal Reserve lowered interest rates to avoid a near recession. Lower interest rates and more lax lending guidelines (due in large part to the government's desire to encourage home ownership) fueled the residential real estate bubble and created a house of cards that eventually crumbled and led to the greatest financial collapse since the Great Depression.

The term "flipper" became a commonly used term during the boom years. In fact, *Flip This House* became a popular TV series on A&E. This series depicted mostly inexperienced real estate speculators buying homes, quickly renovating them, and flipping them for a quick profit.

Flippers were making significant gains after just a few months of ownership. Some speculators bought contracts to purchase condos (typically requiring only 5 to 10 percent down payments) only to sell the rights to close on the unit(s) when the building was completed at some point in the future. Thousands of people (mostly in Miami, Las Vegas, and San Diego) stood in line during the first day of sales for the opportunity to buy a contract. Hundreds of units would sell out in a single day.

A *Business Week* article published in 2005 highlighted the sheer madness of a market gone haywire:

> The latest sign of the Apocalypse: In south Florida, where housing speculation is white hot, some entrepreneurs have unveiled a pair of Internet-based exchanges –USCONDEX.com and CondoFlip.com where individuals can buy or sell condominiums sight unseen. (Dean Foust, "Flipping in Florida" Business Week, July 27, 2005)

Typically, value-add investors buy a property and make improvements to the asset. The value added to the residential property should exceed the cost to make the improvements. If all goes according to plan, the investor sells the property for a profit. During the boom, little was required in terms of adding value except for putting it right back on the market for resale. Prices increased at such alarming rates that many value add investors found that their incremental improvements resulted in exponential growth in perceived market value. It was real estate on steroids. The values grew larger and larger and required less time and effort.

Homebuilders built more homes to keep up with the pace of demand. The largest homebuilders in the country, including D.R. Horton, Lennar Homes, and Pulte Homes, would all peak by 2005. A share of D.R. Horton's stock increased from $3.00 in 1997 to a high of $42.00 in 2005. Pulte Homes, the nation's largest homebuilder, saw its revenue grow from $2.33 billion in 1996 to $14 billion in 2005.

As prices skyrocketed, homes became less affordable, but financing them with low interest rates (or no-interest teaser rates) along with low down payments made it easier to buy. Because most real estate speculators believed that property appreciation would continue unabated, they were willing to pay higher prices just as long as the financing spigot remained in place.

One loan originator I know said, "I never made a loan that Wall Street didn't like." Although the loans were mostly toxic, banks were able to sell them off to the secondary market. In fact, most lenders that sold their mortgage loans assumed very little risk. They merely financed the loans (regardless of whether they believed the borrower could afford it) because they'd profit handsomely from each transaction. If the banks could process more loans, they could make more money. Period. The cycle continued for several years, but the preordained train wreck would eventually force the system to collapse.

By April 2007, subprime mortgages accounted for one-half of all mortgage-backed securities that were being issued. By that summer, the demand for mortgage-backed securities dried up, and the residential real estate market subsequently cratered. By September 2007, the bubble had, indeed, popped, but speculators who failed to liquidated their real estate holdings found themselves between the proverbial rock and a hard place. Prices were quickly declining, and qualified buyers were harder to find.

One of the leading brokers at one of the largest real estate practices in Utah informed me that 35 percent of all residential sales in Salt Lake County were short sales or REOs (real estate owned) in 2010. If you were an average homeowner trying to compete with an avalanche of distressed properties that likely made your home look rather expensive by comparison. I knew people who were current with their mortgage but still desperate to sell. The eventually sold for less than their mortgage balance, and actually had to bring funds to the closing table to pay off the deficiency between the sale price and the outstanding mortgage balance.

## Recovery

With residential values plummeting by as much as 55 percent in some areas, the rent-versus-buy ratios suggest that a recovery is forthcoming. In other words, home ownership is becoming more affordable as the reset in property values takes place. My crystal ball hints at modest growth in residential market by 2012. Once it becomes as affordable to buy as it does to rent, demand will favor home purchases, and prices will stabilize once again. In a healthy market, average home prices do not exceed three to four times the median household income.

*Caveat:* The housing recovery, however, is subject to the health of the overall economy and in particular the rate of unemployment. The rate of recovery is also dependent on the area. Markets that didn't reach a fever pitch such as in Boston, San Francisco, Washington, D.C., Seattle, and New York will fare better than bubble prone markets such as Miami, San Diego, Las Vegas, and Phoenix.

Buyers are swooping in to acquire distressed residential real estate in the hardest-hit markets. Homes that sold for $1 million in 2005 are now trading in short sales for $500,000 or less. Most investors are doing the math and buying when they can achieve a decent return on their investment (from a rental perspective). In other words, an acquisition can be justified if an investor acquires a property at a steep discount, and the existing market rents cover the mortgage, maintenance, taxes, insurance, and so on.

Non speculative investors are buying residential property on the basis of its return as a rental property. They realize that instant appreciation is no longer guaranteed but is an ancillary benefit of ownership. Speculators might settle for a break even scenario with the hope that the market eventually rebounds, and they sell for a profit at some point in the future. Both investors and speculators, however, should plan to hold their properties for at least the next 4 to 7 years before they can realize any significant gains.

As confident as I am that the sun will rise in the east and birds will fly south for the winter, I, too, am sanguine about the prospect that residential home values will recover. It's never going to be like it was during that height of 2005 values again. Values will be based on a percentage of median income. However, we will eventually return to equilibrium – historical increases with annual appreciation in the 3 – 4 percent range.

## Case Study

Ed Henkin is an honest, hard-working home builder and president of Crestmont Homes. His projects can be found in the most prestigious neighborhoods of Boise, Sun Valley, and Jackson Hole. As you can imagine, his homes are some of the finest in the country.

Ed is a fourth generation real estate investor. His great grandmother used a $5,000 settlement to buy her first duplex in New York. She died in 1970 with an estate valued in excess of $1 million.

Ed's Grandfather and father started making second mortgages to New York multifamily investors in the 1970s. During a recession, they began to construct their own portfolio of real estate holdings by foreclosing on some of their nonperforming loans.

Ed grew up in the family business managing several low-income apartment complexes in the Bronx. His Father enjoyed the low end of the business. He once paraphrased Lincoln by stating, "God loved poor people. After all, he made a lot of them."

Ed eventually went to law school but had his heart set on building. In 1988, at the age of 27, he found his first project – an old country farmhouse in the suburbs of Connecticut – that he renovated for his family.

Ed continued to work for his father, managing apartment buildings, but he couldn't make enough money in that position to pursue his lifelong dream of building high-end homes.

Eventually, he moved to Westchester and fortuitously met a gentleman in his 80s who happened to own a significant amount of land in the country. In fact, he was selling lots in a 10-home community but had managed to sell only two when Ed approached him.

He took a liking to Ed and suggested a partnership. Ed agreed to build a spec house on one of the lots and convinced the owner of the land to accept payment after the house sold. As luck would have it, a friend hired Ed to build a custom home for her and agreed to build on his lot.

As he began to build, he started marketing the other eight lots using his custom home as a model. He convinced an all-cash buyer to purchase his second custom home. At that point, he was off to the races. He eventually built five houses in this development and, with a successful track record and the capital he had just earned, he bought vacant land and secured construction financing.

He built a home in Westchester, completed construction, and sold it shortly thereafter. At the time, it was the most expensive spec home sold in the area at $2.4 million.

Afterward, Ed and his family decided to venture west. In 1988, he and his family relocated to Sun Valley.

Fortunately, he was able to buy his first house in cash. His first home was in the first subdivision built in Sun Valley. The house was 5,000 square feet and had "good-bones", but needed a major facelift. Ed managed to complete the entire renovation within six weeks, and his family moved in immediately. He then purchased two more lots in the same neighborhood.

He built spec homes on those two lots and waited for a sale. The real estate market was slowing down, so he decided to place everything he owned for sale, including his primary residence. He waited for three months, but no offers came in. Then, suddenly, he received offers on all three properties.

He sold everything for a significant profit and acquired another home from a builder who was having a challenging time selling. Ed made some changes to the property, lived there for two years, and once again sold at a nice profit in 2004.

At the peak of the market, he sold his next project when it was only 50 percent completed. By 2005, however, Ed realized that something was drastically wrong. Vacant lots were selling for $1,8 million. It cost another $1.8 million to build a structure. He was into the project for a little over $3.6 million (including soft costs). The numbers were becoming unattainable for most buyers. In fact, to illustrate just how ridiculous the market had become, Ed bought a vacant lot for $1.8 million and sold it a few months later with architectural plans (the plans cost $75,000) for $2.6 million!

By 2005, there was a lot more risk involved because the numbers kept getting bigger. Million-dollar projects suddenly became $3 or $4 million investments.

Ed bought land in Jackson Hole, Wyoming in early 2007. He built a 5,500 square foot spec house on a double lot with mountain views. It was completed in early 2010. It's currently on the market for $5.8 million.

In parallel with the Jackson Hole house, Ed partnered with an investor in Sun Valley to build a $16 million estate. Unfortunately, the construction loans matured before he could sell it, and the lender was pressuring him to pay off the balances.

When things started getting bad, he requested a meeting with his loan officer to inform his lender that he was running out of cash. He had done all his business with on bank and had always paid his loans in full. In fact, he was the bank's number one builder during the boom. Unfortunately, the equity in his project was quickly dissipating, and his lender was getting nervous. Refinancing was not an option.

Ed suggested to his lender that he pay them in full when he sells the houses. The lenders suggested that Ed make interest only payments now ($45,000 a month on Jackson Hole home alone) and demanded cross-collateralization on each of the loans.

Unfortunately, Ed did not know how much time would be required to sell the two projects, given the current economic climate. Although Ed had personal guarantees on his loans, the bankers wanted greater security that the loans would be repaid. They requested cross-collateralization with hi primary residence, an increase in the interest rates, and a pledge of interest with other assets that still had equity. This lender was playing hardball.

When you owe the bank a dollar, the bank owns you. But when you owe the bank a couple million dollars, you (sometimes) own the bank. Ed decided to also play hardball, and the bank eventually acquiesced. Ultimately, the lender agreed to extend his loans at the existing rates with the existing terms. Ed was the recipient of a life preserver that would allow him to stay afloat for another 12 months.

When asked about the future, Ed, said, "The future is a bit uncertain. I just want to survive this storm. I know the market will eventually improve and I'll do well."

If Ed is able to sell his properties for the amount he considers they're currently worth, he'll make a decent profit and survive this downturn. If the properties can't be sold before the lenders call in the loans, he'll lose his entire initial investment and be held liable for the deficiency should they sell the properties at a discount in a fire sale.

Ed reiterated his belief in the market and thought that the residential market would rebound by 2012. He's prepared to get right back into the fray by buying a lot at a steep discount and building with a two-year horizon to sell. He can duplicate his initial success by finding a motivated landowner who is willing to partner with him. After all, lot prices are coming way down, and the numbers are beginning to look more attractive again. If the market does correct itself and he's able to sell his properties for a profit and pay off the loans, he could be back in business by 2012 with his first profitable venture in more than 6 years.

Ed expressed a desire to live a simpler life. He needs much less than he has now and wants to live a more modest lifestyle with less overhead. I suspect that anyone who experienced financial hardship during this period will share a similar sentiment. In fact, this is a valuable lesson for us all.

## Case Study

Riley Smith of EWM is a residential real estate agent based in Miami, Florida. Riley is unlike 99 percent of most other Realtors because he's a creative thinker determined to change most of the paradigms established by his industry.

A local investor recently described him as a person "who will put the competition and especially the older and more established but less tech-savvy brokers out of business in this new economy."

Riley started selling residential real estate in 2000. He described the boom years that followed as a constant state of euphoria. It was not easy to obtain listings because properties sold so quickly, and the competition was stiff with discount brokers, so he concentrated his efforts on finding buyers.

"From 2003 to 2006, I was advising my buyers to offer at least the asking price for the homes that interested them. Properties would sell before they were even listed. In fact, we would often write contracts on the hood of a car as house practically sold by themselves back then – sight unseen.

During the euphoric times, the demand outstripped the supply by a significant margin. Riley spent the majority of his time showing his clients around town to find the best house – not necessarily at the best price.

By late 2007, he began to sense that he needed to adjust his business model. At that time, he noticed that the real estate market was slowing down. At that time, he noticed that the real estate market was slowing down. His farm area averaged 45 homes for sale in 2005, but that number increased to 75 and the 100 in 2007. Buyers were pulling back in 2008 and were more reluctant to pay asking prices. He spent time with his team discussing the trends taking place in his industry and decided to act quickly to address the oncoming challenges.

"If you want to survive long-term as a Realtor, you need listings." Riley Said.

To get more listings, he embraced technology to help advance his business and differentiate it from the competition. He started writing a real estate blog to garner attention from a larger audience. According to him, it was the best thing that ever happened, because 75 percent of his listings have originated from his blog during the past two years. The vast majority of his buyers resided outside his farm area because the locals weren't buying during the crisis.

When he launched his blog, it was ranked as the 650th listing on Google. Today, when you Google "Grove Real Estate", his blog was 35th-most-visited real estate site in the country. But he and his wife are required to spend 2 – 3 hours each day writing the blog. "Not everyone can do it. The old-school Realtors don't understand the importance of technology. It requires a lot of work, dedication, and money."

Riley understands that giving the information for free is absolutely essential. The old-timers hold the information close to their vest. They don't release it because they feel that information is their primary differentiator. But what they don't understand is that the Internet already gives most tech savvy consumers the information they need. They just need someone to collect all of the information in one place and interpret the data for them. Whoever can do this for the consumer will do extraordinarily well for themselves.

As Riley likes to say, "The Internet changed my business more than the crisis."

Also, he made a concerted effort to create a unique brand. On each of his for sale signs, the words, "Grove Specialist" appear. Perception became reality, and he is quickly becoming the dominant broker in this area.

Today, Riley spends 80 percent of his time working the business (i.e. paper work, touring with buyers, managing his team, etc.). These days, buyers require significantly more time because they want to tour 35 homes as opposed to just two or three which is all that was necessary during the boom. It can be extremely time-consuming to conduct these tours, so he hired other sales agents to work with his buyers while he continues to oversee their work and develop the platform required to match buyers with sellers.

Admittedly, the completion I s still fierce, but the less competent brokers have left the business, and only good agents remain. Riley has, indeed, prospered during these tough times. Hid indicated that locals are back in the market buying properties again, and sellers want a dynamic Internet presence, so the blog remains his largest source of listings. In 2010 he sold 55 homes, up from 30 in 2006!

One of the areas of opportunity in the residential market my company Boardwalk Consulting is taking advantage of is foreclosed developments. Most developers were caught in a squeeze play when the lending arena got tight. Our first acquisition was a 70 unit town-home development in Draper, Utah. The bank took the property back from the original developer, who was asked by the bank to bring in $1 million dollars to keep the loan in performance. The property values had dropped and the bank was owed more than 75 percent loan to value. We purchased the property at a huge discount and have been able to reset the asking prices on individual units 30 percent less than they were selling three years ago. The investors on this project will make incredible returns, for a relatively safe investment.

## *Key Points from this Chapter*

- History will forever link the current housing crisis to an abundance of easy-to-obtain debt and subprime loans.
- The run-up in residential prices was caused largely by the government's manipulation of the markets and its deregulation of the financial industry.
- Home ownership is becoming more affordable as the reset in property values takes place.
- In a healthy market, average home prices do not exceed three to four times the median household income.
- An acquisition can be justified if an investor acquires a property at a steep discount, and the existing market rents cover the mortgage, maintenance, taxes, insurance, and so on.

# Chapter 15:  Multifamily Housing Units

The housing and financial crises wee disastrous for multifamily operators because foreclosure and failed condo conversion projects added an abundant supply of new units to the existing inventory.  The shadow effect caused by this tsunami of reverted condo units (condos that were reverted back to rentals) had an overwhelming negative impact on the rental market.

Renters had many more options to choose from so rental demand subsequently plummeted, and the increased supply of units depressed rental rates.  I recall my property manager calling me one day in early 2008 informing me of the difficulty he had renting one of my buildings, "Chad, we don't have granite countertops or a swimming pool. Renters expect these upgrades in their units because they're readily available for the same price elsewhere. If we want to be competitive, you might need to upgrade your units or reduce your rental rates."

The failed conversion projects down the street had been upgraded substantially with the intent to sell them as condos. When the market crashed, most developers (or their lenders) were left with empty condos that had to be transformed back to rental units, albeit luxurious rentals. The property owners who owned more traditional units (i.e. those with Formica countertops) were forced to offer prospective tenants free rent and lower rates in order to entice them to lease the less-desirable units. Otherwise, they couldn't complete with the rush of upgraded units coming onto the market.

In my estimate, 2008 and 2009 were the absolute trough years for the multifamily sector. One of my neighbors owns 8,000 apartment units in southern Texas. He is one of the largest owners of apartment units in the entire state. The occupancy rate in his portfolio in early 2007 averaged 96 percent, but by 2009 it had dropped to 87 percent. Meanwhile, his effective rents (rents less concessions) decreased dramatically. However, he, too, agrees that the fundamentals for the multifamily apartment market appear to be improving, and so he is preparing for a dramatic turnaround starting in 2011 and buying up properties at a discount.

## Better Times Ahead

Multifamily will be one of the first real estate asset classes to recover. In fact, 2011 should be a spectacular year for apartment owners. Assuming that the U.S. economy slowly rebounds and the national unemployment rate improves, demand for rental units will soar to new highs. It has taken a few years, but the excess housing supply is being absorbed, and rents are stabilizing. According to the Case-Shiller Index, the bottom of the residential housing market occurred in late 2009 and values have been steadily increasing ever since.

The rental market has already improved and should show signs of steady growth by 2011. The year will usher in a new era with landlords having the upper hand, and it should remain that way for, perhaps, the next 5 years.

The response we receive from our Craigslist rental ads is a fairly accurate (yet non-scientific) barometer for gauging that strength of rental demand in our farm areas. For example, in early 2009 we posted online ads for our rental units in Boston, and on average each one would generate only about 15 responses each week. A year later, we posted the same ads and received twice as many responses during the same time period and rented units twice as fast. Although the demand for rental units will vary from region to region and property to property, the trends (i.e. rental demand, rents, vacancy rates, time to fill vacancies, concessions, and so on) are quickly improving for multifamily property owners.

If retail follows rooftops, multifamily follows jobs. The soft rental market is for the most part a result of the nation's 10-plus percent (maybe over 20% actual) jobless rate. Unemployed tenants have few options other than moving in with relatives or finding roommates to share their homes. That said, fundamentals will change for the better, especially when the labor market gains traction. Labor market experts suggest an increase in employment by late 2011.

Demand for apartments is increasing as people live longer, the echo boomers (the children of the baby boomers) complete high school or graduate from college, and immigrants continue to flock to our country. People need a place to live regardless of how poorly the economy is performing. Also, as individuals continue to suffer financial hardship resulting from foreclosures and bankruptcies, they will turn to apartment units as a more economical housing alternative. With homeowners awash in too much debt, the number of people looking for affordable housing will only increase. For all of these reasons, I am very positive about the prospect for a dramatic improvement in the multifamily sector.

## Supply: Lack of New Product

Very few apartment projects are being built on a national basis. The unavailability of credit for multifamily developers has prevented the construction of many new projects. Multi-family starts have been reduced to a trickle of what they used to be. Fewer than 100,000 units broke ground in 2009 and 2010. The apartment sector has experienced the lowest levels of construction permitting since the 1950s.

Because of the credit crunch, the sector will benefit from an anemic supply of new projects during the next few years. Even as new construction begins in 2011, it will take a few years for those projects to be completed. Supply won't be able to catch up with demand until at the earliest, 2016.

## Demand: Echo Boomers and Hispanics

About 35 percent of the U.S. population depends on rental housing. While the supply of new apartments is halted because of lack of new construction, demand will increase from two main sources: The echo boomer generation and the U.S. Hispanic population.

The echo boomers are expected to be responsible for an increase of half a million new renter entering the market every year from now until 2020, mostly concentrated in the Utah, Nevada, New Mexico and California states. Some experts estimate that the U.S. Hispanic population will grow from 35 million in 1999 to nearly 50 million by 2011. U.S. Hispanics are the fastest-growing segment of our population and will add significantly to the demand for rental units over the next several decades.

If current trends continue, the population of the United States will rise to 438 million in 2050, from 296 million in 2005, and 82% of the increase will be due to immigrants arriving from 2005 to 2050 and their U.S.-born descendants, according to new projections developed by the Pew Research Center.

Of the 117 million people added to the population during this period due to the effect of new immigration, 67 million will be the immigrants themselves and 50 million will be their U.S.-born children or grandchildren. Among the other key population projections:

• Nearly one in five Americans (19%) will be an immigrant in 2050, compared with one in eight (12%) in 2005. By 2025, the immigrant, or foreign born, share of the population will surpass the peak during the last great wave of immigration a century ago.

• The major role of immigration in national growth builds on the pattern of recent decades, during which immigrants and their U.S.-born children and grandchildren accounted for most population increase. Immigration's importance increased as the average number of births to U.S.-born women dropped sharply before leveling off.

• The Latino population, already the nation's largest minority group, will triple in size and will account for most of the nation's population growth from 2005 through 2050. Hispanics will make up 29% of the U.S. population in 2050, compared with 14% in 2005.

• Births in the United States will play a growing role in Hispanic and Asian population growth; as a result, a smaller proportion of both groups will be foreign-born in 2050 than is the case now.

• The non Hispanic white population will increase more slowly than other racial and ethnic groups; whites will become a minority (47%) by 2050.

• The nation's elderly population will more than double in size from 2005 through 2050, as the baby boom generation enters the traditional retirement years. The number of working age Americans and children will grow more slowly than the elderly population, and will shrink as a share of the total population.

## Two to Four-Unit Buildings

While many bottom-feeding investors are searching for single-family houses or condos to acquire for investment purposes, I'd suggest that first-time investors consider duplexes, triplexes and four-plexes.

Two-to four-unit buildings tend to generate more rental income than similarly priced condo or homes. Moreover, properties with four units or fewer qualify for residential loans. Residential loans can be secured with less than 5 percent down (especially if the property is owner-occupied) and come with more flexible terms and condition. By comparison, commercial loans – which require more than 20 percent down at closing – are used for properties with five units or more.

## Time to Buy

It's an ideal time to buy a multifamily property. Interest rates remain low, and prices and cap rates are near pre-1999 levels (where they need to be). Many investors acquired apartment buildings at the peak of the market and are now losing them through the foreclosure process. The disagreement over property values between banks and buyers has created a stalemate in which few distressed transactions took place than originally anticipated. But, the chasm in the bid-ask spread war has finally abated, and more deals are being completed.

Plan to hold any new acquisition for at least 3 to 5 years. Flipping and condoing apartment buildings are no longer a viable exit strategy. Conditions now favor investors who want a long-term investment that generates a decent cash flow and gains value over time.

Traditional value-add strategies to boost a property's NOI must be modified. During challenging economic times, people aren't willing to pay an additional $300 a month for more bells and whistles. Tenants want an apartment in good, safe locations and are price sensitive. The purchase price, therefore, is critical for investors. By minimizing the property's debt, you'll be able to better compete on price.

During this downturn, fortunes will be mad by investing in distressed multifamily properties, so be sure to consider these opportunities very closely.

I will be forming a fund of small investors to pull our money and buy these properties from banks and distressed owners.

## *Key Points from this Chapter*

- Fundamentals for the multifamily apartment market appear to be improving, and so he is preparing for a dramatic turnaround starting in 2011 and buying up properties at a discount.
- Multifamily will be one of the first real estate asset classes to recover. In fact, 2011 should be a spectacular year for apartment owners.
- Demand for apartments is increasing as people live longer, the echo boomers (the children of the baby boomers) complete high school or graduate from college, and immigrants continue to flock to our country.
- Multi-family starts have been reduced to a trickle of what they used to be. Fewer than 100,000 units broke ground in 2009 and 2010.
- About 35 percent of the U.S. population depends on rental housing. The echo boomers are expected to be responsible for an increase of half a million new renter entering the market every year from now until 2020, mostly concentrated in the Utah, Nevada, New Mexico and California states.
- It's an ideal time to buy a multifamily property. Interest rates remain low, and prices and cap rates are near pre-1999 levels (where they need to be).

# Chapter 16: Understand What You Invest In

Real estate brokers generally have particular neighborhoods in which they work, rather than an entire city. Brokers refer to this as a "farm" area. You'd be wise to adapt a similar approach to your real estate investing business. The goal is to become an expert on one specific farm area, roughly 3,000 to 5,000 homes. In some locations, this will be easy because the homes are divided into subdivisions or developments.

Investors encounter significant problems when they don't concentrate on a single farm area, when they chase cap rates out of state, and make "blind" investments, so I make an effort to address this issue whenever possible.

You'd be wise to learn the neighborhood inside and out and become familiar with every detail about it, including home values, schools, zoning, homeowner association restrictions, local shopping and developments, and failed communities.

**Values**—Become familiar with the high and low range of the neighborhood. If all the homes are similar and were built in the same time period, this task should be quite easy. You should be able to rattle off value estimates almost instantly upon hearing a few pertinent details about a particular property in your farm area, such as the style and size of the home. In older neighborhoods (usually 50 years or older), a particular geographical area may have a wide variety of homes, making it difficult to determine values. Novice investors should avoid these areas until they have more experience.

**Schools**—Schools are an important factor for people with families who are considering moving to an area, particularly elementary and middle schools. Get to know the choice of local schools and which ones are most desirable.

**Zoning and homeowner's association restrictions**— Learn the restrictions on building and remodeling as well any homeowner's association (HOA) rules or covenants for the neighborhood that may affect its salability. For example, there may be a covenant restricting how many unrelated people can live in a home within that neighborhood.

**Local shopping and developments**—A new road, highway, or commercial development nearby can affect property values in a positive or negative way. For example, a new shopping center or highway nearby may improve values or be so close as to create undesirable traffic and noise. Get to know what's in the works by following local news and attending local city council and HOA meetings or by visiting the local zoning and planning department.

As an example, let's say that you live in Los Angeles and that the properties you're analyzing don't exceed a 7 percent cap rate. Suddenly, you're made aware of a 10 percent cap-rate. Suddenly, you're made aware of a 10 percent cap-rate on a property in New Mexico. You think to yourself, "It's only a few hours' plane ride away and the property will produce significantly more cash flow than the assets I'm looking at in Los Angeles. I should buy it!"

Big mistake!

That 10-cap deal quickly becomes a 4-cap deal because you didn't know what you were getting into. A local will know the difference between Main Street and Crack Street. One or two blocks in the wrong direction can be devastating.

## *Key Points from this Chapter*

- A local will know the difference between Main Street and Crack Street.
- Investors encounter significant problems when they don't concentrate on a single farm area, when they chase cap rates out of state, and make "blind" investments.

# Chapter 17:  Private Money Lending

Would you lend to a borrower in foreclosure? Or someone looking to buy a large ranch whose value couldn't accurately be determined with a standard appraisal? How about refinancing someone's mortgage so the person can take out hundreds of thousands of dollars in cash?

For "hard money" lenders, it's all in a day's work. These private individuals and small local companies operate where even subprime lenders fear to tread, making loans to the desperate and needy the same way regular banks and brokers service traditional customers. They're harder to find than mainstream lenders and they don't come cheap. But they can help hard-luck borrowers make bad situations better -- and sometimes, they're a consumer's only choice.

There are private investors who, if the interest rate is high enough and the perceived risk is low enough, they will put the money up. Brokers and other intermediaries who arrange hard money -- or private money -- loans go to people who have money to lend and they match them up with people who can't get money any other way.

## Home Buying the 'Hard' Way

If that sounds a little like how the Mob works, don't worry. Hard money lenders aren't loan sharks who break borrowers' kneecaps when they can't repay. At the same time, these lenders aren't your Granny Sue. They charge interest rates and fees that would make conventional borrowers cringe and often base lending decisions on whether there will be enough equity in their subject homes that they can foreclose and still turn a profit. But private money fills a niche in mortgage lending, helping consumers who have specialized needs or too many credit problems to get conventional financing.

"It's across the board," says Brandon Thompson, a private money broker in Denver. "You'll see anything from a $70,000 foreclosure to a half-a-million-dollar loan, where somebody just needs so much cash out and can't verify their income to make it worthwhile for a traditional lender to look at."

For instance, Strickland says one of her hard money lender friends recently did a construction loan for someone building a cabin near Yosemite National Park. Regular lenders balk at such deals because they don't like financing properties in remote locations or those that aren't of standard frame, concrete block or other traditional-type construction. Rural buyers sometimes use hard money loans, too. That's because conventional lenders get antsy about mortgages for properties that derive a substantial portion of their value from the land rather than the house.

Buyers of expensive properties and those who already own such homes and want to cash out large amounts of their equity via refinance loans also turn to private money. So do real estate investors. These buyers purchase properties on the cheap, fix them up and sell them for profit. They use private loans because the loans come with less red tape and restrictions than bank loans.

Borrowers facing foreclosure make up the last major category of hard money customers. When someone misses a mortgage payment, that person usually has some leeway to bring the loan current. But once a 30-day delinquency turns into a 120-day or 180-day one, the lender will usually start the foreclosure process. At that point, the borrower is so far behind that even subprime lenders are reluctant to come in, refinance the loan and start the clock ticking again.

A hard money lender, on the other hand, may be willing to give that person a new loan. The customer can use it to pay off the original lender, gaining enough time to sell the property and find a new place to live. Borrowers who miss payments because of temporary problems, such as a job loss, can benefit, too. They can use the breathing room a hard money loan provides to rebuild their credit. By making payments on time for a year or two, they'll lay the groundwork for a future refinance into a more favorable loan.

"These are temporary fix loans. That's all they are -- to help people get out of a bad situation," says Kirk Johnson, a mortgage broker with Sierra Funding Corp. in Denver.

## If you find one -- be prepared to pay

That said, hard money borrowers face a steep hill to climb. For starters, hard money lenders can be difficult to find. Most operate only within limited geographical areas because they like to see the properties they're lending against personally and know the area around them. Borrowers can try calling around to various mortgage brokers, some of whom have private investors who do hard money loans or know of people who do. Or, they can check their local newspaper's classified advertisement section. Many papers have listings that read something like this: "Can't get a loan? Call Us. Private Money Available."

Customers who can find a hard money lender shouldn't expect to be offered grade-A terms, though. Private money mortgages typically have rates well into the double-digits and often come with several upfront points. People who don't own at least 30 percent or 40 percent of their homes probably won't even be able to get a loan. That's because hard money lenders limit borrowers' loan-to-value ratios so they can still make money off their properties if they have to foreclose. Consumers need to watch out for "loan-to-own" predators, too. They structure hard money loans in such ways that borrowers inevitably fail just so they can take possession of their homes and profit off their sale.

"It's kind of the same rules you get on any loan -- clearly understand what it is you're getting into. Understand what the fees are and what the actual cost of the money is to you," Thompson says. "Be smart."

Despite the pitfalls, lenders say that hard money loans can provide borrowers a lifeline in times of need. Consumers just need to make sure their loans will help get them out of debt, not bury them even further.

"If a property in a subdivision is worth $100,000, the loan-to-value on a hard money loan may be 50 percent to 65 percent, so maybe $65,000 maximum on a first mortgage is loaned against the property" to pay off the old lender who's preparing to foreclose, says Robin Snyder, president of Mortgage Bankers Ltd. in Baltimore.

"That does not mean that that customer can't take the property and sell it tomorrow for $100,000 and reap the benefits of that additional $35,000," he adds. "A person is better off paying 14 percent, or a higher rate than the normal rate of 9 or 10, to keep the property rather than lose it. Or say you don't get $100,000 for it, you get 90. Ninety is better than zero."

## Case in Point

I've been working with a group of investors, where I set up private money loans to help fill a void in the financing markets. By doing this, I solve a problem for people that need money and I help my investors earn 12 to 18 percent on their money per year. I make money through the points paid at closing.

Private financing options are available for personal, investment, and commercial purposes. Private financing simply means you are not dealing with a traditional bank.

Private financing can be obtained from private parties who are also known as Angel Investors, hard money lenders, private equity investors, investment groups, or venture capitalists.

Angel investors make up the largest – and the most flexible group – of private financing options. Angel investors may be relatives, friends, colleagues, or persons as yet unknown to you. If your scope of acquaintances does not yield suitable private financing, spread the word about your project among all of the above, as well as bankers, brokers, business development groups, etc. The right angel investor will for private financing will probably be someone who has some knowledge of your industry. Angel investors may provide a simply loan, repayable with interest and possibly points and a prepayment fee. Alternatively, they may want to take an equity position with your company, taking stock in combination with or instead of interest on the private financing they offer you.

Private equity lenders, aka venture capital firms, can be thought of as a group of Angel Investors providing private financing as a group. Venture capital firms sometimes offer incubators: office suites in which their darling companies (for whom they provide private financing) are housed, watched over, and assisted through the early stages of development. To give private financing groups the returns that their investors are looking for, private equity lenders always want a piece of the action. In exchange for the private financing they offer, private equity lenders take an equity position in your company through stock or some other means and become your financial                                    partner.

Private financing obtained in exchange for stock can be an excellent way to get the initial operating capital needed to start a business, but it can be extremely expensive on the far end. While you will likely not be paying interest in the early stages of your business, you will pay dearly should you become a success.

If you have real estate to collateralize, you may be able to obtain private financing without having to give away an equity position (and a place on your Board, control of your business decisions and all that comes with having a financial partner) by working with a hard money lender, like Boardwalk Consulting. We can provide financing for real estate investment projects, land acquisitions, and construction projects. But, by collateralizing real estate you already own, you may be able to obtain private financing for purposes completely unrelated to real estate. When it comes to hard money private financing, the use of funds is not as important as a clear indication of how the loan will be paid back. Naturally, if you are unable to repay the loan, the real estate collateralized by this kind of private financing will be sold off by the private financing lender, just as traditional banks foreclose on homes when you cannot pay the mortgage.

What does a typical hard money lender make money? That's hard to say because there really is no "typical" transaction. But someone trying to avoid foreclosure might run into the following terms:

- Interest rates: 12 to 18 percent
- Balloon payment: typical, usually due after 6 months to 1 or 2 years
- Loan position: must be a first mortgage, not second
- Maximum loan-to-value ratio: anywhere from 50 percent on up to 70 percent
- Points: 4 to 8 for every year!

Assuming the worst rate and point structure possible, a $100,000 loan could cost as much $8,000 up front and $1,507 a month in principal and interest payments. Borrowers who don't want to end up paying such steep prices should contact their lenders at the first sign of trouble making payments. They may be able to work something out and avoid foreclosure.

## *Key Points from this Chapter*

- Private financing simply means you are not dealing with a traditional bank.
- Private Money Lenders charge interest rates and fees that would make conventional borrowers cringe and often base lending decisions on whether there will be enough equity in their subject homes that they can foreclose and still turn a profit.
- Private financing can be obtained from private parties who are also known as Angel Investors, hard money lenders, private equity investors, investment groups, or venture capitalists.
- Most operate only within limited geographical areas because they like to see the properties they're lending against personally and know the area around them.
- Angel investors make up the largest – and the most flexible group – of private financing options. Angel investors may be relatives, friends, colleagues, or persons as yet unknown to you.

# Chapter 18: How to Add Value to Real Estate

Adding value to income-producing real estate requires a brief explanation of the real estate stack.

On evaluation of all potential acquisition targets, it's necessary to determine whether they are worth your investment capital. The real estate stack is the most basic of quantitative models that allows investors to determine the net operating income (NOI) for any given property. Once the NOI for an income-producing property is determined, the value can be derived, and that asset then can be compared to any other real estate investment opportunity.

Before you consider spending time touring a property, you should create an analysis of the asset based on the stack. Given your finding from this simple financial model, you can determine whether the property warrants a site tour.

**Real Estate Stack ( or Operating Statement)**

Potential Gross Income (PGI)
(Less) Vacancy and collection (V&C)
(Plus) Other income  (OI)
(Equals) Effective gross income (EGI)
(Less) Operating expenses (OE)
(Equals) Net operating income (NOI)
(Less) Debt service (DS)
(Equals) Before-tax cash flow (BTCF)

# The Stack Explained

The potential gross income (PGI) of a property is the amount of annual rental income a property should (under ideal conditions) generate.

Assume that we have a 100 unit apartment building and that each unit rents for $1,000. The PGI equals $100,000.

Vacancy is shown as the average percentage (of the PGI) that the property is expected to remain vacant throughout the year. Collection losses amount to uncollected rent from existing tenants. Let's assume it's 5 percent or $5,000.

Other income (OI) amounts to revenue that is not based on unit rental income. OI could be generated from garbage rental, pet fees, rental of storage space, and so on. If 100 unit owners pay $100 a year toward storage space, OI= $10,000.

Effective gross income (EGI) is the amount of revenue you expect the property to produce each year. It is PGI less V&C plus OI:

$100,000 - $5,000 + $10,000 = $105,000

Operating expenses (OE) include all the property related expenses attributed to ownership. Some common operating expenses include advertizing, insurance, taxes, repairs, reserves for replacements, maintenance, utilities, and so on. Operating expenses do NOT include debt service.

Assume $40,000 in operating expenses.

Net operating income is the Holy Grail for all investors because it represents the basis for comparison, assuming debt is not a factor. It represents the property's income before paying debt and income taxes:

Annual debt service (DS) is the sum of all the mortgage payments for the year. The annual debt service includes both the principle and interest payments on an annual basis.

Before tax cash flow (BTCF) represents the gain or loss realized by the investor for the year. It does not consider taxes on that income.

The property analysis would look like this:

**Annual Property Operating Statement**

| | |
|---|---|
| Potential gross income | $100,000 |
| -Vacancy and collection | (5,000) |
| + Other income | 10,000 |
| Effective gross income | 105,000 |
| -Operating expenses | (40,000) |
| Net operating income | 65,000 |
| -Debt service | 30,000 |
| Before tax cash flow | 35,000 |

Now that you understand how to create a property income statement, you're prepared to better comprehend how to add value to your investment property. If you plan to sell the property, the NOI must be maximized, to achieve the highest possible price at the time of the sale. To maximize NOI, you must improve all the factors that influence NOI including: PGI, V&C, OI, and OE.

Increase the rents, and NOI goes up. Reduce vacancy and collections, and NOI increases. Increase storage fees or start charging for Internet access, and NOI can climb. Reduce operating expenses (OE) by negotiating a rate reduction with your insurance carrier, and NOI will be positively affected. Do all these things, and watch how the NOI improves and the property's value soars.

Let's assume that the average cp rate in your area for the asset class is in question is 8 percent.

If you property's NOI is $65,000, the value of the property is $812,500 ($65,000/.08).

Now let's assume that you spent the past year working on your property so that NOI increases by $20,000 to $85,000.

The property is now worth $1,062,500. That's a $250,000 increase in value.

Concentrate like a laser on the stack and make improvements in every category that affects NOI, and your property will realize what's referred as "forced" appreciation. Value-add deals are properties that can increase in value based on incremental improvements by ownership.

If holding the property for its cash flow over the long term is the goal, you should execute a plan to increase NOI (as discussed above) along with a strategy to reduce your annual debt service obligation. There are three principle ways to reduce annual debt payments:

1. Refinance the property to a lower rate.
2. Pay down the mortgage with larger equity payments and refinance
3. Pay off the mortgage and eliminate debt payments altogether

If you're a real estate investor, then you're in the value-add game. Your job is to think of new ways to create additional value so as to consistently maximize NOI and cash flow.

If it's new construction or buying a property with a lot of vacancies, most commercial agents don't factor in the lease-up costs and holding costs. Do a real-world analysis where you look at those cost.

## Case Study

Barry Anderson is the principal of Anderson Real Estate, LLC. He's a real estate investor and broker based in Las Vegas, Nevada. Barry buys vacant land (especially in areas shadowed by Wal-Mart) and develops the land for use by national retailers. The amount of rent that retailers are willing to pay largely determines what he can pay for the land. He won't buy land unless he has a lease in hand. Barry specializes in locating sites that retailers want and can afford. And he is very good at adding value to land by securing the requisite permits, rezoning the land (if necessary), and developing properties for national high credit tenants. Let's say that a 2 acre lot is worth $1 million. How much is that 2 acre lot worth if Walgreens would construct a 15,000 square foot store and pay $50 a square foot NNN (the tenant pays for the taxes, insurance, and common area maintenance) or pay an equal amount for the ground lease?

That property would generate $750,000 NOI (assuming all expense are paid by Walgreens). Using an 8 percent cap rate, it's worth over $9,000,000.

When times were good, Barry's model worked like a charm. The market, however, changed for the worse in 2008. Walgreens started cancelling projects that were approved at the local level, and other national retailers also pulled back.

"Changing our model wasn't the best course of action because my strategy still works in good times and bad. In bad times, it just happens a lot slower," Barry Says. Single-tenant, build-to-suit projects are fee-based, so there's always a profit to be earned if he can match the right real estate with the right tenant.

Barry feels that future opportunities lie in the existing product because, "New shopping centers aren't penciling out. 2011 should be better than 2010. I'm going to sift through all my deals and start over in 2011."

## *Key Points from this Chapter*

- If holding the property for its cash flow over the long term is the goal, you should execute a plan to increase NOI (as discussed above) along with a strategy to reduce your annual debt service obligation.
- Concentrate like a laser on the stack and make improvements in every category that affects NOI
- To maximize NOI, you must improve all the factors that influence NOI including: PGI, V&C, OI, and OE.
- Once the NOI for an income-producing property is determined, the value can be derived, and that asset then can be compared to any other real estate investment opportunity

# THE FUTURE

# Chapter 19: Credit Markets

U.S. banks have lost billions during the past few years. They made questionable loans to individuals who didn't have the ability to pay them back. In fact, most subprime borrowers lacked the credit, income, and assets to qualify for their loans. Nevertheless, the banking community bent over backwards to provide unqualified borrowers sufficient debt to purchase homes they could ill afford. Lenders also encouraged homeowners to extract additional capital from their properties (as if the property was a piggybank) in the form of home equity loans. This additional capital fueled consumer consumption and debt to greater heights. Lenders also provided heavily leveraged loans to real estate speculators who acquired income-producing properties with very little of their own equity. During the boom, nearly every loan applicant qualified for a mortgage, business line of credit, or home equity loan. Credit was plentiful and easy to obtain, and over leveraging became an acceptable business practice.

Unfortunately, the lax lending practices were the cause of the housing crisis and subsequent financial meltdown. Too much mortgage debt caused the U.S. economy to fall into the worst economic recession since the Great Depression. As loans reset and homeowners lost their jobs because of the faltering economy, debt-laden Americans realized that they couldn't keep up with their poor spending habits. Ultimately, lenders were left with a sea of bad loans that could never be repaid. The crisis served as a wake-up call to the banking industry. If it wants to survive this fragile economic crisis, it had better change its ways.

Banks that have managed to survive the residential housing collapse are now bracing themselves for an aftershock –failing commercial property loans. Lenders are anticipating a second wave of defaults before conditions improve. Because of this concern, banks have tightened their lending standards and are adhering to significantly tougher qualifying standards. These new lending guidelines will probably remain in place for the foreseeable future.

It is unlikely that lenders will return to the irresponsible activity that was so common during the boom years (at least not for a long time). Instead of financing a property with a 90 to 100 percent LTV, lenders are requiring 20 to 30 percent down. They are demanding that buyers have sufficient equity in a property so the, if values continue to fall and the borrower stops making payments, the banks won't be forced to liquidate at a price less than the balance owed. In other words, lenders will mitigate their losses requiring borrowers to come to the closing table with more of their own cash.

In many other instances, banks have stopped lending altogether. For example, one of the most common complaints I hear from shopping center owners is that their prospective tenants can't secure financing to build out their space. Small businesses are finding it difficult to obtain loans even working capital. Retailers with profitable business models (even during the recession) and successful track records cannot find a bank to lend them the capital needed for expansion. Construction loans are impossible to find, and few lenders will consider making a loan unless the borrower has a significant down payment, sufficient collateral, an exceptional credit rating, and a lengthy track record of success. That's precisely why cash is king right now. If you don't require debt to make acquisitions, you're in an enviable position to by at historically low prices. If you don't have the readily available cash but still want to acquire real estate, then you must find equity partners who want to invest in your projects. Make them limited partners and give them a preferred return on their capital. In other words, they get paid before you get paid. Family, friends, and business partners can provide the equity you need to get started. Equity partners provide the down payment, and are allocated a percentage of the annual cash flow and equity in the deal. Try to avoid raising additional debt from outside sources, though, because you don't want to be burdened with extra payments beyond the principal mortgage. If you succeed, your limited partners will receive a nice return on their capital and likely invest more in your next project.

Perhaps the phrase "no money down" will eventually disappear from the American lexicon. If you're a budding, you investor who wants to get into the real estate game, but you don't have a job or savings, please don't turn on the television after 1 a.m.. I don't want a late night real estate infomercial guru to convince you that buying properties and making millions is possible if you have absolutely no savings, source of income, or capital to invest. No-money-down investing is just bad advice. The exception, of course, is finding equity partners (as discussed above) that provide the capital while you provide the sweat.

Americans spent during the boom as if there was no tomorrow. There was an absolute disregard for living within a budget and investors failed to honor the tried and true fundamentals of real estate investing. Rather, they bought on speculation, expecting property values to increase regardless of the changing times. The rules of the new economy will challenge our society to live and invest within their means – and that will surely benefit everyone.

## *Key Points from this Chapter*

- Cash is king right now.
- Construction loans are impossible to find, and few lenders will consider making a loan unless the borrower has a significant down payment, sufficient collateral, an exceptional credit rating, and a lengthy track record of success.
- If you succeed, your limited partners will receive a nice return on their capital and likely invest more in your next project.
- Equity partners provide the down payment, and are allocated a percentage of the annual cash flow and equity in the deal.
- If you don't have the readily available cash but still want to acquire real estate, then you must find equity partners who want to invest in your projects.
- No-money-down investing is just bad advice.

# Chapter 20:  The No-Debt Alternative

Private equity groups, Real Estate Investment Trusts (REITs) and other institutional investors claim it's impossible to achieve their desired internal rate of return (IRR) without leverage.  They typical return accepted by most institutional investors ranges from 17 to 25 percent. U.S. based institutional firms rarely acquire real estate unless they can apply leverage to their financing.

Allow me to illustrate the power of leverage:

- Purchase price: $1,000,000
- Equity (cash in): $200,000 (20 percent)
- Debt: $800,000
- Assume the property increase in value by 10 percent (or $100,000) in 1 year and is immediately sold. The sales price is $1,100,000.
- Profit: $100,000 (not considering closing costs, legal, brokerage, finance fees, etc)
- Return: 50 percent (100,000/200,000)

If the buyer made an all-cash purchase, the return would amount to only 10 percent. ($100,000/$1,000,000). Note: This is a very simplistic example used for illustrative purposes only.

I am not questioning the merits of leverage in real estate investing. However, I have begun to doubt its efficacy for non-institutional investors who are consistently wiped out by the ebb and flow of market cycles. Because real estate is not liquid and it takes time to sell, the average real estate investor tends to lose a good portion of his equity when the market collapses (which is approximately every 8 to 12 years). Family fortunes are decimated, and dreams are dashed. There are an inordinate number of people who lost everything in this downturn, including their homes, boats, second homes, cars, college savings for their kids and perhaps, most important, their motivation to start over again. Even some smart, experienced investors lost what they had spent a lifetime building.

Most investors tend to think that more properties means more money and a great net worth. However, this mindset doesn't always lead to the most optimal long-term strategy. Bigger doesn't always equate to a better financial position for most non-institutional investors. A sounder strategy is to buy good real estate assets in great locations from motivated sellers. Then renovate the properties, lease them at market rates, and pay off the mortgages as soon as possible. Buy with the intent to hold for the next 30 years. When you finally pay off the mortgages, the properties will then generate an impressive cash flow each year.

Would you like to create a significant passive income stream from your real estate holdings to sustain your family through retirement and pay your kid's and maybe even your grandchildren's college tuition? Keep in mind that owning 50 buildings that are highly leveraged is usually not nearly as profitable as owning 10 buildings free and clear of debt.

A mortgage is like a deadly cancer. Get rid of it. Extract it as soon as possible. A prudent financial goal is to increase your cash flow by paying off your mortgages. I have a good friend of mine who owns seven properties in California. He says that he could significantly increase the size of his portfolio if he wanted to, but he owns the buildings mortgage free. The cash flow from his small real estate empire is more than ample to provide a nice lifestyle for his entire family. He no longer needs to work and has found greater balance in his life.

Another acquaintance of mine owns 10 very successful restaurants in Seattle. He bought the buildings where his restaurants are located and paid off the mortgages years ago. He's 70 years old now buy carries two cell phones with him at all times. He works like a dog. "But for what?" I ask him, "how much do you need? One day you'll have a heart attack. You have enough money and sufficient cash flow to sustain yourself as well as the next few generations of you family. Stop working so hard and enjoy life a little – enjoy life a lot!"

Historically, mortgage institutions have encouraged investors to take a leveraged position in the real estate market. Unfortunately, too much leverage makes an investment highly prone to fail. The rules of the new economy dictate that you rethink this outdated investment philosophy. Acquire real estate with less leverage and pay off those mortgages. The most successful investors I know buy real estate with a minimal amount of debt and make a concerted effort to pay down those mortgages as soon as possible. Take a more conservative approach to investing, and finance with low leverage and pay down the existing debt as quickly as possible. Cash is, indeed, king, and cash-flow is maximized when servicing debt is no longer a factor.

In general, the people I know who are raised without a safety net tend to work much harder in life than those who were raised with a safety net. Having the capacity and desire to consistently work hard is really a gift. Many people don't have the ability to dedicate themselves 100 percent to their chosen vocation. For instance, if you feel that everything can be taken away from you if you fail and no one (parents, uncles, aunts, family friends, etc.) is there to get you out of trouble should you stumble, survival becomes a basic instinct that forces you to work much harder than everyone else. Regardless of your particular station in life, work hard toward your goals – as if you didn't have a safety net and as if failure were not an option. Paying off those mortgages helps too.

## *Key Points from this Chapter*

- The most successful investors I know buy real estate with a minimal amount of debt and make a concerted effort to pay down those mortgages as soon as possible.
- Having the capacity and desire to consistently work hard is really a gift.
- Historically, mortgage institutions have encouraged investors to take a leveraged position in the real estate market.  Unfortunately, too much leverage makes an investment highly prone to fail.  The rules of the new economy dictate that you rethink this outdated investment philosophy.
- A mortgage is like a deadly cancer.  Get rid of it.
- Owning 50 buildings that are highly leveraged is usually not nearly as profitable as owning 10 buildings free and clear of debt.

# Chapter 21: The Economic Recovery

An astute real estate investor I know recently commented, "The economy will recover when the press declares it so, and not a day earlier."

The media's predictions, however, regarding the economic recovery are rather mixed at this time. Many analysts have declared that we reached the bottom in mid- to late 2009, while others claim it will take more time. Some say the recovery will be "V" –shaped (although that's quickly not becoming an option) while other claim it will be "U" shaped. The real pessimists predict that shortly after the economy shows signs of recovery, it will be followed by a downturn with high inflation and, perhaps, another recession. An "N" shaped recovery – up, down, up.

According to a recent New York Times article, "60 percent of Americans think the country is heading the wrong direction, and the same percentage believes that the United States is in long-term decline." Eight million jobs were lost during the past few years, and it's going to be a long climb up the economic ladder to get those jobs back. According to a recent *New York Times* article, "More than 80 percent of economists say the United States won't regain all the jobs lost in the recession until 2015 or later..." (David Brooks, "Relax, We'll Be Fine," April 5, 2010)

Admittedly, this economic meltdown has been the worst financial crisis since the Great Depression. But rest assured that an economic rebound will eventually occur, and investors who choose to align themselves on the side of prosperity will act before the media begin writing about the Great Recovery. After all, contrarian investors will have acquired much of the low-hanging real estate fruit in your farm area by the time the media decide to stick their necks out and publicly declare the end of the "Great Recession".

## Housing Values and the Recovery

Few economists and housing experts would object to the notion that the recovery of the housing market is paramount to the health of the overall economy. In fact, until housing values bounce back, the recession (in one form or another) will likely continue to plague our nation.

The pace of the housing recovery will vary throughout the country because homes in cities such as

Miami, San Diego, Las Vegas, Phoenix, Los Angeles, and Detroit will require significantly more time to regain their value than less hard-hit cities such as Boston, New York, Washington, D.C., and Seattle. Home prices have decreased by as much as 55 percent since the peak of the market. It might take 5 to 10 years for many homeowners to regain the equity lost in their properties. Some property owners might have to wait even longer. Millions of homeowners who owe more on their homes than the homes are currently worth will be confronted with years of negative equity, thereby increasing their risk of foreclosure and adding to the burgeoning supply of distressed real estate that already exists.

Even after home values stop falling, it will take time for some property owners to generate any significant equity. Carrying a property with negative equity will affect the consumer confidence of millions of people. I estimate that as many as 35 percent of property owners' home loans are "under water".

Nevertheless, there are some signs that the housing market is strengthening. Home sales have increased, and the available inventory on the market is gradually shrinking. As mentioned, the latest Case-Shiller report suggests that housing prices bottomed out in 2009.

The overall health of the economy and in particular the housing market is dependent on several factors, including, interest rates, inflation, the credit markets, consumer sentiment, the labor market, and so on.

## Jobs and the Recovery

A significant reduction in the unemployment rate will help sustain a strong recovery. But even when the economy does begin to rebound, the unemployment rate might not realize a meaningful improvement because of the enormous number of layoffs during the past few years. And once individuals find gainful employment, their depleted savings will leave them more vulnerable than ever before. You should expect modest employment growth during the next few years (a jobless recovery), as most businesses remain reluctant to add additional head count to their payrolls until there's a clear indication of a turnaround.

Companies will avoid hiring as long as possible. Maximizing productivity will be the primary focal point for most firms in the coming years. Because of this, existing employees will be required to be more productive and perform more work than ever before.

Nevertheless, there are indications that employment is improving. Job postings (online listings of job opportunities) rose by nearly 20 percent in 2010, according to Indeed.com. In particular, employers are becoming more bullish in towns such as Boston, San Francisco, New York, and Washington, D.C.

## Consumer Confidence and the Recovery

If employment numbers increase in a meaningful way, consumer confidence will rise, and spending will follow. Homeowners will still need to reconfigure their finances after absorbing sever declines in the values of their properties. A psychological reset will need to occur whereby the debt-laden ways of the past are discarded, and a new sense of financial responsibility and accountability will be imprinted on the minds of the next generation. Households will save more than they have in the past, and eventually consumer confidence will be restored. It will, however, take a generation to forget what happened in the meltdown.

## The Credit Crunch and the Recovery

The constricted credit markets will impair business and investors for years. Business will no longer have access to easy loans and unlimited credit. Homebuyers and real estate investors will be confronted with significantly more challenging financial restrictions and will be required to contribute more of their own capital to their acquisitions.

With little or no equity remaining in millions of homes throughout the country, homeowners will be unable to extract capital (in the form of home equity lines) from their homes. This, for the record, is one of the most beneficial outcomes of the economic bust.

Commercial real estate is the next shoe to drop, and lenders are sensitive to the next wave of defaults. They are reining in lending because they realize they're not out of the woods yet. Unfortunately, if banks aren't actively lending, the recovery will take longer to gain momentum.

# Interest Rates and the Recovery

Some economists are concerned that heavy government spending along with higher deficits will eventually force interest rates to increase. As interest rates rise, the cost of borrowing for both consumers and businesses becomes more expensive, thereby delaying the recovery.

# Reasons to Be Optimistic

During the next 40 years, our country's population is expected to increase by 100 million people. By the 2050, 400 million people will reside in the United States. This magnitude of population growth, assuming estimates are accurate, will increase exponentially – the demand for apartments, single family homes, retail centers, offices, hotels, and industrial buildings.

Keep your eye on home prices, GDP growth, the unemployment rate, inflation, retail spending, and the consumer confidence index. There is a host of other economic indicators, in my opinion, of the economic recovery. On a less scientific basis, I also like to speak with local furniture store sales people. Furniture sales (or lack thereof) are an economic barometer during tough times. They tend to be a fairly accurate indicator of the relative health of the local markets.

We are a country with enormous untapped potential. Regardless of what the pundits might want you to believe, America is still a dynamic and vibrant nation with a bright future ahead of it. Your hard earned investment dollars are well spent in a place with political stability, relatively fluid financial markets, a rising population, a productive and entrepreneurial workforce, and a history of successfully rebounding from challenging economic times.

Investors willing to embrace risk during precarious economic times will be rewarded. However, once those market risks have subsided, the potential returns will diminish as well.

## *Key Points from this Chapter*

- Eight million jobs were lost during the past few years, and it's going to be a long climb up the economic ladder to get those jobs back.
- The constricted credit markets will impair business and investors for years.
- Investors willing to embrace risk during precarious economic times will be rewarded. However, once those market risks have subsided, the potential returns will diminish as well.
- During the next 40 years, our country's population is expected to increase by 100 million people.

# Conclusion

*"The flaws in human nature are such that this sort of crisis will occur again. Maybe not in a long time, but greed will cause a financial crisis again."*

Alan Greenspan

Times have changed. The economy has changed. Financing has changed. Real estate has changed. Therefore, your strategy for investing must change.

The terms "housing bubble", "housing crash", and "subprime mortgage" may not have been part of your everyday vocabulary a few years ago, but they certainly have become commonly used phrases today.

The U.S. economy experience the worst economy recession since the Great Depression. Subprime lending and too much debt caused the meltdown, but Wall Street financiers and the federal government perpetuated it. Fortunes were made during the housing boom, and fortunes have been subsequently lost during the housing bust. Too much lending to people who ill could afford the heavy debt pushed the system over the edge. Unlike the last major economic collapse, when large commercial real estate investors were mostly affected, the average "Joe Citizen" this time around lost his home, savings, and job.

Every time you think you know the rules of the game, the rules change. Now the economy and the real estate markets are shifting into a new phase. The economy will reset, and the rules of engagement will be altered. In the new economy, banks will be more cautious and reluctant to lend unless the risks are significantly minimized. Consumers will be more cautious and spend less (and maybe even save more) until they feel more secure about their jobs. Household debt was reduced by approximately $600 billion since the fall of 2008, according to Equifax. That's proof that households are paying down their debt (i.e., household deleveraging), and it's a positive sign for increased spending power in the future.

The recession, by many estimates, ended in late 2009, and economists appear to be increasingly bullish about the housing market in the next few years. Warren Buffett even predicted the recovery of the residential real estate market by 2011 by stating, "Prices will remain far below bubble levels, of course, but for every seller or lender hurt by this, there will be a buyer who benefits. Indeed, many families who couldn't afford to buy an appropriate home a few years ago now find it well within their means."

Nevertheless, many borrowers will have a difficult time securing mortgages because of tougher standards being imposed by banks. NINJA (no income, no job and no assets) have been dismissed as an unethical and unacceptable way of conducting business. Not only will you need to provide evidence of a job, good credit, and a stable source of income, you will be required to make a sizeable down payment for your purchase (this goes for commercial buyers as well). New federal laws that prohibit lenders from interacting with appraisers will reduce fraudulent appraisals. It's going to be much more difficult to obtain a loan in the new economy.

High loan-to-value (LTV) ratios coupled with secondary financing are also relics of the past. Our country was addicted to leverage, but we are now in a period of deleveraging. Property owners who borrowed too much and need to refinance will be required to make substantial equity payment toward their debt to reduce their LTV ratios. Exorbitant leverage mad popular in the United States, however, is not an acceptable practice throughout the entire world. In fact, one of my good friends represents a real estate investment fund in Bogotá, Columbia. This firm has no tolerance for purchasing properties with more than 50 percent leverage. In other words, it would need $25 million for a $50 million purchase. Because of Columbia's historical boom and bust cycles, investors in that country realize that they must buy with a significant amount of equity. Most investors who survive the longest and thrive for several decades tend to be more conservative with their real estate financing. They either tap into their own cash reserves or work with well-financed equity partners to acquire real estate with a reasonable amount of debt. They fully understand the treat of using too much debt, so they structure their deals accordingly.

It's back to the basics with sound lending practices, larger down payments, and conventional fixed loans. And don't plan on banks relaxing their lending standards for quite some time.

"Pigs get fed and hogs get slaughtered," one of my good friends said, who heads up the special assets department at a large private equity fund. In other words, if you're a pig, you want to eat but not get so fat as to become a candidate for the slaughter mill. Politicians who get too greedy can suffer a similar fate at voting time, and the same holds true for investors. If your overleveraged and wait too long in the cycle to make more money (because of greed), you will eventually get slaughtered.

Both investors and lenders used little discretion. Banks made poor decisions and investors got caught up in the euphoria. Residential market lending has reverted back to the old rules of lending: 720 credit scores and 20 percent down – and it's a problem if the property's appraisal determines that it's worth less than the purchase price. In order to make money in this market, it really will take money! There's no free ride anymore.

According to my friend in special assets, "Investors will need a longer term plan to make $1 million. It's going to be much more difficult to make a million in 12 months. Investors will need to hold properties for their cash flow and pay down debt. There will be some appreciation, but that won't be overnight. They'll be able to sell for a profit down the road but there are no quick deals anymore. There are no instant home runs. Instead, there's a lot of hard work and a 7 to 10 year horizon to exit.

## When to Buy

When I first got into real estate sales at the age of 19, there was a veteran agent in his late 40s that had a private office. In this agent's office was a sign that was hung above his desk that stated, "Lord, please give me one more recession and I promise not to waste it this time."

Real estate can be a tremendous investment vehicle if you are able to sustain a long-term vision, especially if you buy at depressed prices and have patient money. You need to invest when the sky is falling, and in many parts of the country it has been for years. By the time the media claim that the economy is recovering, the market has already adjusted, so don't wait to read about it. Novice investors jump into the fray when real estate investing is most popular, but the true professionals enter when everyone is frightened by its predicted collapse. That's precisely why novice investors usually get burned, but the experts make a killing.

With debt not readily available and billions of dollars worth of commercial loans maturing, retail and office properties will soon experience their worst years since 1990. Refinancing of commercial mortgages will be nearly impossible unless there's significant equity in the property. But because valuations have come down so much, most loan-to-value covenants have been broken and refinancing won't be an option for many owners. The entire commercial sector will soften during the next few years and this will present even more opportunities for savvy investors.

There is undoubtedly an abundance of opportunities to purchase good cash-flowing properties in your farm area. There is also a tremendous opportunity to acquire foreclosures at undervalued prices. However, distressed investing will require extensive due diligence and research on your behalf to avoid overpaying in a market that's continuously evolving. As I've stated, "You make money when you buy!" Buying well today improves the likelihood that you'll sell profitably in the future.

# Real Estate Investing is a Local Business

A partner at a large accounting firm I do business with told me that a high-net –worth client of his had five commercial loans with his local bank. The firm had always been current on its loans and never posed a financial risk to its lender. The president of this lending institution called him a few months ago to inquire about his appetite for acquiring a property that would complement his existing portfolio – but at a steep discount to its existing debt and well under market value. Because he had been a loyal customer who had always paid his mortgages on time, he was on the bank's priority list to call when distressed deals presented themselves. The moral of the story is that you need to establish strong ties with local lenders, and always make sure they know you are ready to buy.

# Success and Optimism

There is a multitude of reasons to explain why some entrepreneurs make it and others fail. You can have two restaurants next door to each other, with the same access to raw foods and labor. One restaurant will thrive and the other will fail. Being an entrepreneur is not easy. Some entrepreneurs just fall short of their goals. Success is largely determined by individual characteristics that propel the best entrepreneurs to the pinnacle of achievement.

Ultimately, making money in real estate is less dependent on geography, recessions, recoveries, buyer or seller's markets, REOs, short sales, the credit crunch, lax lending standards, or your personal cash reserves or lack thereof. The most important factor in determining your success is (you guessed it) YOU.

Your success is determined by whether you're a pessimist or an optimist. After all, this book has shown you some ways to make money in real estate, but it's entirely your responsibility to execute a plan and achieve your desired outcome.

Every successful person I know has one trait in common: Each is utterly consumed by positive thinking, and they are all supremely optimistic people. They take absolutely nothing for granted. They don't assume the world owes them great wealth, fame, or success. Life is not fair, so they set their expectations accordingly.

Ultra-successful people go out and earn their keep every single day. They tend not to act entitled and never stop moving forward to achieve their goals. They encounter challenges and difficulties along the way (just like you and me), but they never falter. That's what sets them apart from everyone else. They preserver when others give up. They always find a way to work through problems that otherwise might impede their progress. The word "can't" just isn't part of their vocabulary.

I wish you amazing success with the endeavors you are pursuing and even though I don't know you, I feel like you are going to be a success. Good luck!